CAMBRIDGE LIBRARY COLLECTION

Books of enduring scholarly value

Philosophy

This series contains both philosophical texts and critical essays about philosophy, concentrating especially on works originally published in the eighteenth and nineteenth centuries. It covers a broad range of topics including ethics, logic, metaphysics, aesthetics, utilitarianism, positivism, scientific method and political thought. It also includes biographies and accounts of the history of philosophy, as well as collections of papers by leading figures. In addition to this series, primary texts by ancient philosophers, and works with particular relevance to philosophy of science, politics or theology, may be found elsewhere in the Cambridge Library Collection.

The Presuppositions of Critical History

This work combines two early pamphlets by F. H. Bradley (1846–1924), the foremost philosopher of the British Idealist movement. The first essay, published in 1874, deals with the nature of professional history, and foreshadows some of Bradley's later ideas in metaphysics. He argues that history cannot be subjected to scientific scrutiny because it is not directly available to the senses, meaning that all history writing is inevitably subjective. Though not widely discussed at the time of publication, the pamphlet was influential on historian and philosopher R.G. Collingwood. The second pamphlet is Bradley's critique of Henry Sidgwick's *The Methods of Ethics*. Sidgwick was the first to propose the paradox of hedonism, which is the idea in ethics that pleasure can only be acquired indirectly. Published in 1877, this work is divided into three parts, treating Sidgwick's definitions, arguments, and his view of ethical science.

T0345380

The Presuppositions
of Critical History

F. H. BRADLEY

CAMBRIDGE
UNIVERSITY PRESS

CAMBRIDGE UNIVERSITY PRESS

Cambridge, New York, Melbourne, Madrid, Cape Town,
Singapore, São Paolo, Delhi, Tokyo, Mexico City

Published in the United States of America by Cambridge University Press, New York

www.cambridge.org
Information on this title: www.cambridge.org/9781108040440

© in this compilation Cambridge University Press 2012

This edition first published 1874
This digitally printed version 2012

ISBN 978-1-108-04044-0 Paperback

THE PRESUPPOSITIONS

OF

CRITICAL HISTORY.

BY

F. H. BRADLEY,

FELLOW OF MERTON COLLEGE, OXFORD.

OXFORD.

JAMES PARKER AND CO.

1874

PREFACE.

THAT the following pages should not go before the public without an apology I am very sensible. Their matter I fear is unsatisfactory, and their manner worse; but no alteration that I could make would be likely to improve either. The reason why these reflections are printed at all is my wish and hope that they may be instrumental in leading some more capable person to clear up and dispose, once and for all, of a subject which ought to be disposed of.

The barbarous title of the following pages anticipates their method, and to some extent their conclusion. Their method consists in taking the existence of certain facts for granted, and in endeavouring to discover the conditions of that existence. These conditions by their absence annihilate the facts; and hence the facts involve them, take them for granted, presuppose them. And the conclusion is that, as the facts *have* presupposed the principle unconsciously, so now in judging we must proceed upon that principle consciously, and use it as a canon.

The subject of critical history is not so narrow as at first sight it might appear. There is no history which in some respects is not more or less critical. No one in the world thinks or could think of inserting into a history of the world *all* the events which have ever been handed down, precisely *as* they have been handed down. But if this is not done, if we exclude or alter or rationalize to the very smallest extent, then we have criticism at once, and we ought to know what criticism means.

That question being asked, it became obvious that critical history must have a criterion, and the next matter was to find that criterion. It seemed equally clear after a time that the canon of history was —the historian. This result comes naturally from the consideration of particular historical practice (and in this respect as in others let me acknowledge how much I am indebted to Baur's 'Epochs of Church History-writing,')* as also from reflection on the psychological aspect of the general question. The historian as he is is the real criterion ; the ideal criterion (if such an antithesis can be pardoned) is the historian as he ought to be. And the historian who is true to the present *is* the historian as he ought to be.

This is the main thought in what follows, and, in order to reach such a conclusion, it was necessary to meet antagonistic doctrines at every stage, as well as objections which sprang up in my own mind continually. I have tried so far as possible to avoid wearisomeness, but have not succeeded; and, what is worse, I fear that I may not have succeeded, even as the cost of weariness, either in removing the objections I myself have raised, or in anticipating those which may occur to the reader. I think that in order to have attained a satisfactory result, the whole subject of probability and certainty ought to have been investigated. To this task I felt myself unequal, and my conclusions are hence to some extent precarious.

The preface is already out of proportion to the performance, but I am forced to say a word in conclusion on the application of any-

---

* I may mention here that Von Sybel Gesctze der Historischen Wissens, and Droysen's Grundriss der Historik are very brief and well worth reading, though they came to me too late to be of much use.

thing set down here to religious questions. For what I have said I am answerable, but for nothing that any other person chooses to conclude. The view I have put forward is this, that every man's present standpoint ought to determine his belief in respect to *all* past events; but to no man do I dictate what his present standpoint ought to be. *Consistency* is the one word that I have emphasized. I can not help it if any one thinks that the conclusions of this essay are reconcilable with only one belief or disbelief. I can only say beforehand that such a man's opinion is not mine. These conclusions, I think, are negative only of a breach between the worlds of the present and the past; and to point out where such a breach exists was not my business, still less my business to express an opinion on the relative truth and falsehood of existing religious beliefs.

If we meddle in any way with the history of certain times, we must touch the element or a part of the element, in which hitherto the Christian principle has brought itself home to the religious consciousness. And to a person who identifies the element with that which exists in it, or who believes that the truth of a principle is to be found at the beginning of its temporal developement, such modification will doubtless appear an *all*-important matter. That it is important I do not question. I know that it is so. But I know this also, that the extent and generally the nature of the influence, which a modification of history must exercise on religious belief, is a subject on which it is remarkably easy to come to a conclusion, and extremely hard to come to a right one. Courage to express one's views has long ceased to be a virtue. Except where persons are concerned, there is no merit in possessing it, and it is on the fair way to become a vice. And, especially where religion is involved, there is one courage it is well to be free from, the courage to utter one's (mere) opinions.

iv.

All that I have left to say* is that whatever below may be of use to any one here does not belong to me, except in the sense in which a man's debts are his own. My debt is owing in Oxford, and my use of what I have borrowed is very far from the approach to a payment.

* I ought to mention that in Note A. I have tried to bring the subject home to the general reader, while Note E. is not meant for the general reader at all.

SUMMARY.

Critical history involves two sides or elements, 'objective' and 'subjective' (3—4). False account of the relation of these two sides (4--5) ; refutes itself (6).

What is a fact for history? Not a simple datum of the senses (7); but a complex totality (8), a judgment (9), and more, a conclusion (10). This illustrated (10—12).

Testimony, as experience of others, rests for us on inference from our own experience (12—13). Illustration of this (14).

All history has a 'prejudication.' What is this? (15) Omnipresence and uniformity of law. History must assume this and so must science (15—17). Freedom of will no objection to it (18).

But what does uniformity in history mean ? It means that all historical facts are subject to inference from the present world (18—19).

Objection to this. 'The present world itself depends on testimony' (20). Yes! but the critic's present world ought not so to depend (21).

Further objection. 'Then no testimony which goes beyond the analogous can be received' (22). Yes! it can; but only on certain conditions (22—23). Where testimony *must* fail to take us beyond analogy (25—26).

Is historical testimony of this latter sort ? (26). What is *historical* testimony ? Hard to say (27—28). We must take it to have three characteristics (28—30)

Once more, can historical testimony establish the non-analogous ? (31) If it does not go beyond probability, No! (32—33). Reasons why it can not go beyond. (33—35).

[Objection. 'This only applies to *existing* historical testimony. But history, as a science, is to rest on scientific evidence.' (36.) Why this will never be. (37—38).]

Result at present obtained (38). Application of this result to historic material. Criticism must be partly negative (39), and absolute (40). Criticism stands towards tradition in four attitudes (41—43). Criticism not bound to explain everything on pain of retiring from the field (43—45).

PRESUPPOSITIONS OF CRITICAL HISTORY.

IN the world the mind makes for the manifestation of itself, and where its life is the process of its own self-realization, there the action and the knowledge of it are children, the hours of whose bringings-forth are never the same, and whose births are divided. Alike in the life of mankind, and in the developement of the individual, the deed comes first, and later the reflection; and it is with the question, 'What have I done?' that we awake to facts accomplished and never intended, and to existences we do not recognise, while we own them as the creation of ourselves. For a people only in the period of their stagnation, for a person only when the character and the station have become fixed for ever, and when the man is made, is it possible to foreknow the truth of the fresh achievement; and where progress has its full meaning, and evolution is more than a phrase, there the present is hard, and the future impossible to discern. Unborn in the substance of the present there lies, it is true, and there lives that future: but the unborn is hidden as yet from the light, and the womb is secret, and the presage doubtful; and the morning of the child's naming is divided by many days from the darkness of begetting and the night of travail.

The sudden act of a moment is unveiled, it may be, to the gradual consciousness of advancing age; and there are seasons again when the slow drift of years comes home with a flash of sweet or sombre revelation; or it may be again that of these experiences neither is given for the time to humanity.

Neither the projection nor the recognition of reality are always the work of an hour; for there are periods when gathering tendencies and accumulation of changes copy their alterations in an altering reflection, when another day dawns through longer twilight, and another world more slowly steals on the sense, with its images so strange yet so familiar, and another man wakens through uncertain recollection to the same and yet to a new self-consciousness.

It has been thus with the growth of the critical mind. It fought in the name of another, and not in its own name; it has conquered before it set itself to the battle; and it was first in the making of its realm that it grasped the secret of its mission. The feeling of itself as power came before the knowledge of its purpose, and the passing of the power into act disclosed to it first its own nature. But the advance of its action was gradual, and the consciousness of itself was of equal growth, and with a tardy revelation followed the steps of a slow developement.

Within the memory of to-day it has been that historical criticism has asserted, and has made good an unabated claim; and with a sudden tide of success has risen to the consciousness of its unabridged mission. With the knowledge of itself it now knows also the purpose of its existence, and the reality which, in the field of its endeavour, belongs to itself and to itself alone.

Criticism has become self-conscious: but to be aware of its aims and the character of its work is one thing; it is another thing to attempt to comprehend the conditions of its being, and the justification of its empire. Such justification it is which historical criticism now mostly needs; for that criticism cannot, except by its actions, justify itself. Confined as it is to one limited sphere, to reflect on the grounds of its existence is for it to pass beyond that sphere; and the principles which regulate its practice are thus, because it cannot account for them, its presupposition.

This is the subject of that which follows in these pages, and these pages will, so far as possible, be limited to this alone. Nor, however much at first sight it may appear so, will it be found an easy task to investigate the principles of critical history. It is a hard matter, because neither do we know at the outset what we mean by 'critical,' nor shall we learn even at the end what history in general is, nor even assure ourselves of the fact of its existence. We here have enough, and, it may be, more than enough of considerations on history and on the 'science of history,' with its actual or possible or impossible reality; but the question, 'When we use the word history what do we mean by it?' is, it would seem, too simple or too trifling a problem to stay the course of our 'advanced thinkers.' And yet the man who, feeling himself unequal alike to support that position or that title, is contented simply, so far as he can, to think, knows all too well that question, and knows it as involving the most difficult problems which philosophy can solve or discuss. Such a man, whatever may be his school, or whatever his his principles, will not I know take it amiss in me that I confess at this point my inability, and seek to impose neither on myself, nor on his understanding, nor on the ignorance of the public. And so to begin——

It has been often remarked that, by whichever of the terms now in use we express it, history has still a double meaning. 'Geschichte' does not simply stand for 'Was geschieht,' and ἱστορια would not merit its name were it nothing beyond the inquiries of the historian. Starting from different sides these words are extended, each to the same totality, by a broad, or if any one pleases, by a loose signification.

It might I believe be maintained plausibly, and perhaps even with serious conviction, that these two elements, that of events in time on the one side, and, on the other side, that of recollection in the mind, were in history necessarily united; in this sense that a bare series of momentary occurrences cannot contain that without which history has no right to be named as history.

But such a discussion lies beyond our subject, and we must be be content here both to assume an historical past of humanity, in the absence even of a recording subject, and to leave the assertion of a merely 'objective' history of Nature to stand or to fall untouched by us.

We do not question that history apart from the historian does exist; and contrariwise we must take it for granted that there is no such thing as history which is merely 'subjective,' or, in other words, that whatever is 'created' by the historian is not in a proper sense history at all.

For that history as a whole has been so 'made,' that in it we have nothing but a series of projections of present consciousness in the form of a story of past events, from time to time gathered up or abolished in a larger and more inclusive projection—this has, so far as I know, been upheld by no sober-minded man, nor could be : it is only the exceptional writings of particular periods of which such an account can be given, and scarely even then without any modification.

But, be this as it may be, we refuse the name of history to such a production, and we assume that though history (Geschichte) may exist, where the writing of history (ἰστορια) does not exist, yet, where there is no real past, there there is properly speaking no historian also, nor any writing of history.

In what follows we have nothing to do with history as it is not for the historian : history presupposes in its title of 'critical,' the presence alike of the so-called 'objective' and the so-called 'subjective' elements; and it is only as involving both that we intend in future to use or to discuss the word.

In this sense (to touch at length on our proper enquiry) history stands not only for that which has been, but also for that which is ; not only for the past in fact, but also for the present in record ; and it implies in itself the union of these two elements : it implies, on the one hand, that what once lived in its own right, lives now only as the object of knowledge, and on the other hand that the knowledge which now is possesses no title to existence save in right of that object, and, though itself present, yet draws its entire reality from the perished past.

Stated thus the facts would appear to force us to a grave consideration; but problems are hard to those alone who make them so, and to account for the conjunction of so diverse attributes has seemed (it is well known), and still seems to the earliest reflection, no difficult task. The explanation is simple. Knowledge is the reception of outward impressions, and it is but natural that the copy should resemble and reproduce the original. And if that, which, independent of any act of judgment was first learned, be in like manner simply and honestly written down, surely this copy of a copy is still, undistorted by so transparent a medium, and true to the mould its original has shaped, the living imprint and the faithful though uncoloured likeness of the full reality?

Such is the view natural to the uncritical mind, and according to this history has no presuppositions, and indeed can have none: her province is to recall, and not to construct; she wishes to take the truth as it is, not to make it what it should be; and she demands from the historian the surrender of his judgment to the decree of the ages, not the projection of his desires and fancies into a region for ever passed from the limit of creation, dead to the action and the storm of life, whose tranquil expanse no breath of thought can ruffle, and where the charm is broken when the mirror is moved.

The theory is simple, and it may be pleasing, but it is no more than a theory; and could we, as we cannot, be blind to the difficulties which beset it from within, yet it is doomed to perish, for in its own practical application it exposes its own falsity and reveals its own illusion.

We ask for history and that means that we ask for the simple record of unadulterated facts; we look, and nowhere do we find the object of our search, but in its stead we see the divergent accounts of a host of jarring witnesses, a chaos of disjoined and discrepant narrations, and yet, while all of these can by no possibility be received as true, at the same time not one of them can be rejected as false.

But the consciousness, for which testimony is the reproduction of a passive print, is at this point not resourceless. 'The pure rays of truth,' we are told, 'are discoloured by the various media through which they pass, and it is the task of the historian to correct the refraction of one medium by that of another, and in this manner to arrive at the bare and uncoloured reality.' But the historian, if such be his mission, is not and cannot be merely receptive, or barely reproductive. It is true that he may not actually add any new material of his own, and yet his action, in so far as he realises that which never as such has been given him, implies a preconception, and denotes in a sense a foregone conclusion. The straightening of the crooked rests on the knowledge of the straight, and the exercise of criticism requires a canon.

This is not the only difficulty which historical writing in its practice brings to the theory of passivity. There remains on the contrary another of equal weight. When the records of a bygone age have been all collected, and, so far as possible, brought into harmony, yet at this point the task of history does not cease. Writer after writer in rapid succession takes up the never-exhausted theme, and, where no new fact is left to discover, there still remains the ceaseless endeavour more and more thoroughly to apprehend the old material, the passion of the mind to be at home in its object, the longing to think the thing as it is in itself, and as all men have failed to think it before. With every fresh standing-ground gained by the growth of experience, with every rise of the spirit to a fuller life comes another view of the far-lying past from a higher and a new level, and a fresh and corresponding change in the features of the object recognised. Impotent to deny the exist-ence of these facts, and powerless to explain them, the uncritical consciousness refuses to advance, or advancing loses all hold on reality. It is forced to see in the place of its reproduction an origination, in the place of its witness a writer of fiction, in the place of its fact a theory; and its consistent issue is the barren scepticism which sees in history but a weary labyrinth of truth and tangled falsehood, whose clue is buried and lost in the centuries that lie behind.

An issue consistent, and indeed for a space necessary; but in-evitable to none except those alone who through helplessness and doubt have set their faces towards the truth. To the double-minded seeker, to the man who, though fain to win, has no heart to stake his possessions, in *this* sphere at least there is *no* inevitable conclusion. He justifies his belief in anything by his right to be convinced of nothing; yet for a present pleasure he foregoes his inheritance, and buys his immunity at the cost of slavery.

In view of the futility of such an outcome, nor finding a solution in the metaphor of a crude reflection, unable to remain in the doubt of scepticism, or to sink to the dogma of despair, it remains to us once again to take up the question abandoned thus by the un-critical mind, and, with patience if not with hope, at least to attempt to exhibit it in a truer form. The heading, 'Presuppositions of Critical History,' expresses briefly the doctrine which is the opposite of the uncritical, and anticipates the result that a history without so-called prejudications is a mere delusion, that what does everywhere exist is history founded upon them, and what ought to exist is history with true preconceptions consistently developed throughout the entire field.

But, to take up the problem from the beginning, we must return once more to the uncritical mind, and to its doctrine or its metaphor concerning historical tradition. The ultimate element in the field of history is, as before remarked, presented and necessarily presented to itself by that stage of reflection as a so-called 'fact,' the imprint of which is on the part of the witness passively received and preserved: that which brought itself to the observation is subsequently repeated, or written down as so observed, and, in the absence of direct falsehood on the part of the narrator, remains as a simple and indecomposable material. This is the theory of simple reproduction, a view to be met with not solely in the world of common sense: the psychology of the people has made it its own, and consecrated it in the name and with the title of philosophy, and still we are assured with the complacency of an absolute certitude that in perception the mind is passive, and that the final elements of knowledge are the facts conveyed through the senses.

Into the fulness of the problem raised by sensationalism, into the truth which underlies this 'metaphor now hardened into a dogma' we are not prepared, nor indeed is it necessary to enter here. We will content ourselves on the general question with the remark, that in the *act* of perception it is no doubt true that the mind is at the same time passive. But to say this is to say one thing, and it is quite and altogether another thing to talk of sensations (in the signification of bare feelings) as though in themselves, and apart from the activity of the mind, they existed as objects of consciousness. That is to *assert* that a mere feeling is sufficient to constitute by itself the minimum required for knowledge and reality; and the proof of this assertion has been, is, and ever will be wanting. It *cannot* exist since the proof or even the assertion is a sheer self-contradiction; and it is a self-contradiction for the following reason. An assertion, and much more so a proof, is intellectual; it is a judgment which implies the exercise of the understanding; and the terms united by the judgment must therefore fall within the sphere of the understanding. They must be objects for the intellect, and so, in a sense more or less entire, relative to the intellect; in a word intelligible. But the essence of mere sensation was the entire absence of the intellectual, and hence to make one single affirmation with respect to sensation, as sensation, is to treat as relative to the understanding that which is supposed to exclude the understanding; and this is a contradiction.

To pursue with the reason an object which when found is to be irrational, to think the opposite of thought while fixed as opposite, to comprehend the incomprehensible yet without transforming it—such is the task of that which calls itself the 'philosophy of experience.' It is the pursuit of a phantom for ever doomed to fade in our embraces, a mocking shadow beyond the horizon of our grasp, known to us as the unreality of all that we can hold, and whose existence must perish at the threshold of human possession.

Yet let this be as it may. We are not concerned to ascertain the nature of that which may be regarded as the minimum of fact in general. The object of our enquiry is history, and specially here the ultimate material of the historical field; and we wish to know not what makes any fact, but what makes an historical fact, and what it is without which nothing can rightly be called by that name. We have to enquire in short what it is that in history and for history is required for the existence of its historical matter, and what it is that, be it what it may be in itself, yet can never enter as as a member into the narrative of the past.

The facts which exist for critical history are events and recorded events. They are recorded, and that is to say that, although the work of the mind, they now at any rate are no mere feelings, nor generally the private contents of this or that man's consciousness, but are fixed and made outward, permanent, and accessible to the minds of all men. Failing to be thus they have failed to be for history, and history can never be for them. And they are events, and that is to say that each is no simple and uncompounded unit, but contains within itself a motion and a passage, a transition and a connection between elements, relations, the members of which may be distinguished though they cannot be divided. They are recorded events, and that means that, though fleeting in themselves, they are yet made stable; though divisible in time, they are regarded as wholes; and though the offspring of the mind, they are still independent and real.

Such are the characteristics of historical facts considered in themselves. We must regard them now in their relation to the individual witness or recorder. Let us view them as the objects of his consciousness, and ask what are they? and what function of the mind corresponds to them?

To solve this problem in a short space is scarcely practicable, and to ensure brevity we must be willing here to seem, it may be, contented with assertion.

They cannot be mere feelings. A chaos of sensations has no unity, and hence cannot properly be *called* a succession; nor, even when re-collected as a sequence of feelings in me, can it yet express an outward change in things. In a word from feeling to the record of an occurrence there is, and there can be, no *natural* passage.

If we recall the characteristics of the narrated event, in the first place it will be clear that they presuppose in the mind both association and recognition of association: association as that which separates (distinguishes), and at the same time conjoins; and recognition as that which is aware of the divisible unity as a concrete whole. They require the action of that faculty which separates the subject from the object, and one thing from another thing, while it yet remains the bond of their unity. In a word they testify to the presence of judgment. A feeling *is* at most; it is neither real nor unreal, true nor false: but every occurrence has or has not taken place, and every judgment professes, although it may fail, to express the actual.

The historical event (in our limited sense of the word history) involves in the first place a judgment. It is 'objective,' it is distinguished in itself, and yet it is a whole.

But in the second place it involves much more than what we call a simple judgment. If we take the simplest historical fact, and reflect on the complex nature of the transition it attempts to express, it is clear to us that we are concerned with a number of judgments, the multitude of which wearies our attempts at analysis. And it is not less clear that these many judgments are united, and, as it were, resolved in a single judgment which answers to the whole event.

This one judgment comprehends in itself the many judgments; it must be looked on as their result, or in other words it is a conclusion.

The historical fact then (for us) is a conclusion; and a conclusion, however much it may appear so, is never the fiction of a random invention. We bring to its assertion the formed world of existing beliefs, and the new matter of a fresh instance. They are grounds for our position, and we know them as such, or at least we may know them. For everything that we say we think we have reasons, our realities are built up of explicit or hidden inferences; in a single word our facts are inferential, and their actuality depends on the correctness of the reasoning which makes them what they are.

Such is (or seems to be) the constitution of the narrated event; and, if its statement is a paradox, it is at least no new one. The evidence which the result lacks here will perhaps not be required by the reader; but in any case, so far as what follows is concerned, he must look for at most a further illustration.

To resume the discussion. In the case of the most straightforward witness deposition to the most ordinary circumstance contains in every instance the recognition of the previously known under fresh features and with new particulars: it involves inferential judgment; inferences of substance and attribute, of cause and effect, and, if the inference is false, the fact is unreal. It is matter of the most ordinary experience that the mediated and complex should appear immediate and simple. We see what we perceive; and the object of our perceptions is qualified by the premises of our knowledge, by our previous experiences. Not only to the child is the novel picture identified with a familiar image, but to each and all of us an uncertain shape is defined on a sudden as a particular object, or the tremor of a feature conveys the emotion of the soul— and all by what seems at the moment a mere communication of the senses.

Yet it is a proverb that in everything a man may be mistaken: and the reflection (when we do reflect) upon our errors brings home to us the conviction, that we are wrong only because we judge, and that, without this condition of both error and truth, existence would be for us impossible.

If we go to the strongest facts, to the best attested events as they are proved in our law courts, we are forced still to admit that there are no facts as to which mistake is impossible; and in every case the mistake rests upon a mistaken inference. But, as we have said, it is the merest illusion to suppose that the entire abstinence from, or the total removal of inference, is a guarantee for certainty and truth. The best witnesses are those who from long habit have attained to comparative infallibility in their judgments; the testimony even of a child on familiar subjects is of value; but there may be events to which its deposition is worthless, not because it makes inferences, but because it fails to make them, or makes them wrongly, and not because we can not trust its eyesight, but because we can not rely upon its reasoning.

It is natural at this point to object that in cross-examination the lawyer has a means for removing the witness's conclusions and arriving at the sensible facts. This to a certain extent is true; a witness can be forced (in certain cases and down to a certain point) to recall and unwind the coil of inference which has made his events what they are. But to confine him to the facts of sense is to reduce him to a condition of impotence. If the man is to speak to anything, in the end the examination is confronted with a judgment, which can not be called a sensible fact, and which yet defies its analysis; because, though there must be a ground, yet that can not be recalled, since it never, as part of a conscious reasoning, was explicitly before the consciousness. Here the process must cease, and the existence of the fact rests upon the veracity of the witness in other respects, and the correctness of his judgments on general subjects. But with every precaution the best witnesses may be mistaken; there exists no testimony entirely secured from error; and the possibility of wrong evidence implies the possibility of false reasoning; nor in any case is it explicable except on the assumption that testimony to the simplest circumstance involves, and is what it is by reason of an inference.

If it is thus where every safeguard exists, how will it be where there are none? And if the ultimate legal fact in its very nature is inferential, can we not say with still greater truth that in the realm of history we have and can have no facts whatever which do not hold in their essence and depend for their existence on inferential reasoning?

The correctness of the isolated event as recorded rests upon a theory, and the recorded train of circumstances which makes a narrative is a still wider theory, which must depart yet farther from the fact as imagined to consist in passive sensation, and must imply, together with its greater possibilities of truth and falsehood, the increased existence of active combination. We can not recall accurately what we have not rightly observed, and rightly to observe is not to receive a series of chaotic impressions, but to grasp the course of events as a connected whole.

It is a fact not to be lost sight of that our memories are certain only because corrigible, and have become trustworthy solely through a process of constant and habitual corrected recollection; the correction being in every case the determination of an order by fixing its elements in their proper relations, and its result a mediated sequence of phenomena.

We have considered the primary historic material, both as single occurrences and as series of events narrated by an original eye-witness, and what we have so far seen is this, that in the field of history it is impossible to free ourselves from reasoning, and that in every case that which is called the fact is in reality a theory. The identification (so far and in this sense) of theory and fact, is the end of that stage in our discussion which we have just accomplished, but we are far as yet from our final result. 'Your conclusion,' it will be urged, 'be it never so true, is far from justifying the historian in assumptions or presupposition.

'Let it be with the facts and the narratives as you will; but they come to the historian as testimony, as the experience of another, and, whatever they be in themselves, yet for him, as he has them, they are facts: and in any case all further reasoning concerning them is frivolous.'

The doctrine might be stated with a show of plausibility. Will it bear the test of a practical application to our daily life? I think that to accord our impartial ear indifferently to things probable and improbable, to things true and false, and for no other reason than because we do not see with the eyes and hear with the ears of others, is, if we consider it, a strange and extravagant demand.

I am sure that we might search long and in vain through the lives of those who profess such a creed for any the smallest exemplification of it; and the reflection might occur to us that there are better illustrations of a belief that all things in general are equally credible, than the violent affirmation of the dogma that some things in particular are absolutely certain.

The common experience of reasonable beings bears us out in the assertion that we do not believe without a reason; that the fact asserted by another remains in its position, as an asserted fact, unless we have some cause to take it as true, and to make it a part of our own world: and further that this reason and ground is a reasoning (if not always a rational) judgment, from the possibility or likelihood of the event, and the character of the witness. The distinction between our individual experience and testimony as the experience of others, is not a distinction which can have the smallest tendency to modify the conclusion we arrived at above, viz., that all our history is matter of inference.

The distinction moreover is to a certain extent illusory. If to say that 'all knowledge comes from experience' is to utter no more than 'an empty tautology,' then it must be but a similar tautology to assert that all experience is personal experience. The teaching that it is impossible for a man to transcend his consciousness is not unfamiliar to our ears; and we have learnt the lesson (important or otherwise) that we can only know the things which we can know, and that our world will never be wider than the world which will be ours.

It is a doctrine which often stands for no more than a ground for disbelieving and believing whatever we please; but here, as against the separation of testimony from experience, it has its significance. The experience of others has no meaning for us except so far as it becomes our own; the existence of others is no existence for us if it is not in our world that they live. If we know that other men are, we know it by an inferential judgment: and it is by a similar judgment that the matter of their testimony becomes ours. Both they and it can be nothing to us but parts of our experience; are made parts of it by an inference, and have no validity and no guarantee beyond that inference. To deny this is to state the opposite of a tautology, is to fall into a self-contradiction.

If nothing is ours which is not in our experience, then testimony, if known by us, must be so included: and at this point a familiar illustration may perhaps be excused as tending to throw some light on the preceding statements.

I have met, as I imagine, a friend in the street to-day, and I note it as a fact that A. has been seen by me; but this is an inference, the theory on and of certain supposed recalled sensations. I am told on the next day by an eye-witness that A. died yesterday; my inferences from the character of the witness, the recognition of a narrative of the death written in the handwriting of A.'s relatives, lead me to believe this. It is now a fact that A. died yesterday; but this fact is again my inference: it is I that have made it a fact for me, and, in case there has been a conspiracy to deceive me, it is not fact, but a false judgment of mine. What is now to become of the fact of my meeting with A.? That depends on my reasoning, on my general beliefs, on my presuppositions. It may be a fact that I have seen an apparition, or the fact may be now an hallucination; but both one and the other are inferences. It would be possible to proceed much further. I might learn that a real man like A. was present at the place and time. A mistake as to persons is now the fact. And it is useless here to urge that the visual sensation at the given time is the ultimate reality; because, in the present application, we have seen that, let it be never so actual, history can admit no such reality into its sphere; and in the second place there need not have been such visual sensation at all. For, if there were no reason to suppose the presence of any real man, and if an hallucination were hardly possible in my case, the fact might be that my memory was disordered, and that I dated too late a former meeting with A. In short, the fact varies with my judgment, and my judgment must always be based upon and fall within my own experience.

The history then (to proceed), which is for us, is matter of inference, and in the last resort has existence, as history, as a record of events, by means of an inference of our own. And this inference furthermore can never start from a background of nothing; it is never a fragmentary isolated act of our mind, but is essentially connected with, and in entire dependence on the character of our general consciousness. And so the past varies with the present, and can never do otherwise, since it is always the present upon which it rests. This present is presupposed by it, and is its necessary preconception.

History must ever be founded on a presupposition; and the scepticism which saw in the succession of historical writings a series of fictions, where the present was transported into the bygone age, was thus and so far justified: but the insight into the ground of the partial justification will exhibit, I hope, the source of the general mistake.

Paley protested against that which he called a 'prejudication.' We have seen the reason why every history is necessarily based upon prejudication; and experience testifies that, as a matter of fact, there is no single history which is not so based, which does not derive its individual character from the particular standpoint of the author. There is no such thing as a history without a prejudication; the real distinction is between the writer who has his prejudications without knowing what they are, and whose prejudications, it may be, are false, and the writer who consciously orders and creates from the known foundation of that which for him is the truth.

It is when history becomes aware of its presupposition that it first becomes truly critical, and protects itself (so far as is possible) from the caprices of fiction. But what, then, it will be asked, is the presupposition of criticism?

The answer is not far to seek. It is plain from the whole of what has gone before that the ground of criticism is that which is the justification of inference; and an inference, it will be admitted, is justified solely on the assumption of the essential uniformity of nature and the course of events.

Critical history assumes that its world is one, and that in that world it exists, and has but to demonstrate the existence of itself. Its demand is that the judgment which we found to be implicit in every historical fact become explicit, and that the whole sequence be consistently and rationally mediated. As intelligence, criticism seeks the object which already is in itself intelligible, and it realises itself, if at all, in the form and the character which belongs to itself alone. In a word the universality of law, and what loosely may be termed causal connection is the condition which makes history possible, and which, though not for her to prove, she must none the less presuppose as a principle, and demonstrate as a result worked out in the whole field of her activity.

To this extent the characteristics of history are the characteristics of (natural) science, for both carry into the particulars an anticipation which the particulars have already realised in implication: and the reason of this is, that for both the fact can exist so far only as already possessed of attributes conferred on it by virtue of the principle, and can oppose the principle by no means but its own self-annihilation.

'Science,' we may be told in answer, 'is founded on experiment and not on a presupposition.' 'The fact of the existence of scientific experiment proves,' we must return, 'the existence of an absolute presupposition, which it can be said to found, only because upon that itself is already founded. We base our action on that which our action itself supports and testifies to. Unless upon the assumption of the exclusion of all interference and chance, no one could say that an experiment was of the smallest value. The man of science cannot prove his assumption beforehand; he knows that as a fact his science exists, and that there are certain conditions necessary to its existence, and he troubles himself little (if at all) with the possibility of the falsehood of his assumption.

Can science testify to a breach of the law which forms its presupposition? This would amount to a contradiction in terms; it would be an observation based upon a rule to prove the nonexistence of the rule; it would be a deductive reasoning in which the conclusion would be a negative instance against the leading major premise. No experiment could prove that A (if isolated) was at one time followed by B, at another by C; because the very apparatus of the proof rests upon the absoluteness of the principle —that is to say, the judgments necessary to support the facts of the hostile experiment are self-annihilated in virtue of the experiment's supposed result. Science may retire from the field altogether, but, while in its field, it has no choice but to remain supreme.

That science should rule its facts seems disputable only so long as we suppose the facts to be something independent. But the truth is on the other hand that every scientific observation and experiment involves an inference true or false, and known to be true solely in virtue of the law. The simplest possible datum which is matter of science is no mere atom, but expresses and depends upon connections in things to which the judgment if true must conform. But to know that relations of thoughts express relations in things is impossible except on the formal or virtual assumption of the absolute stability of these latter relations, and the consequent assurance that a false judgment is the result of a false inference in me, and not of a shifting connection in the world. Science does and must control its facts, and an opposing fact is self-condemned because in every element the principle is already involved.

We find then that, as starting from a conception which it cannot prove, natural science is, in this sense, hypothetical, and exhibits in detail the truth of its hypothesis. Returning to history we must ask if in this respect it corresponds to science?

That history and science (always in its English limitation to physical science) present no diversity, we are far indeed from suggesting. Unlike most branches of science history can create no experiments; and its subject-matter (we must take it for granted here) is not the same as the matter of science. The difference is wide, but, so far as the point above dwelt on is concerned, both science and history we find to be agreed, in this namely, that a fact which asserts itself as (loosely speaking) without a cause, or without a consequence, is no fact at all, and no better than a self-contradiction, for the reason that, while professing to exist, it abjures the sole ground of actual existence.

But there is an objection which at this point we are certain to encounter. We shall be told that the volitions of man are uncaused, and that hence the doctrine put forth above falls to the ground. Whether, strictly speaking, causation retains a meaning when applied to the will, we need not to enquire. 'Causation' we use throughout in the loose sense which it bears amongst us. And into the question of the relation of freedom to law we are not obliged here to enter. For our present purpose however we may thus dispose of the difficulty.

If the freedom of the will is to mean that the actions of man are subject to no law, and in this sense irrational, then the possibility of history, I think, must be allowed to disappear, and the past to become a matter of almost entire uncertainty. For, if we are precluded from counting on human nature, our hold upon tradition is gone, and with it well nigh our only basis for historical judgment.

We find however that the contrary is every day assumed as certain, and that where the weightiest interests are at stake, and as long as criminals are executed in many cases by right of what comes to a construction from the laws of human action, so long will there be at least no practical necessity for the discarding of historical evidence in favour of the doubts, or perhaps the dogmas, of any man.

Thus much at present then seems to be clear—that critical history must have a presupposition, and that this presupposition is the uniformity of law. And we have accomplished here yet another stage of the present enquiry.

But this, we shall be told and rightly told, is much too indefinite. No one now asserts the existence in history of events without a cause or a consequence, and the real point at issue is to determine more narrowly the character of the general principle. 'Uniformity,' we shall be told, 'is an empty phrase; similar causes are doubtless followed by similar effects, but in the varied field of history there are causes unlike those which present themselves in our present experience, and which consequently imply the presence of unfamiliar results.' Upon this difficult point it is necessary to attempt to come to a clear understanding.

We have seen that history rests in the last resort upon an inference from our experience, a judgment based upon our own present state of things, upon the world personal in us; and that this is the sole means and justification which we possess for holding and regarding supposed events as real, i.e. as members in and of our universe. When therefore we are presented, as it were from the outside, with so-called 'historical facts,' the like of which seem to stand in no relation to all that we have now in heaven or on earth; when we are asked to affirm the existence in past time of events, the effects of causes which confessedly are without analogy in the world in which we live, and which we know—we are at a loss for any other answer but this, that (so far as at present we can see) we are asked to build a house without a foundation, or with our instruments construct a work which can come into no connection with those instruments. And how can we attempt this without contradicting ourselves?

When further we reflect upon the range and diversity of our present experience, its width in respect to the different stages of developement which it exhibits, and the continual and growing success of its attempt to find an unity in all that variety; then we find it still more impossible to accept, as the real past of our own real world, this riddle of an outer sphere, fallen amongst us down from heaven, and written in a foreign tongue.

Our difficulty is this—we are asked to affirm the existence in history of causes such as we can find nothing analogous to now in our present experience. On the other hand, it is only from our knowledge of what is, that we can conclude to that which has been; and, this being so, how can we first infer from the world to the existence of historical evidence within the world, and then, starting from that, proceed out of the world, when all the time we are unable to stand except upon the basis of the world?

As we reflect, the conclusion is borne in on us (perhaps prematurely), that, upon the strength of historical evidence, to assert within the sphere of history the existence of any causes or effects, except on the conviction that there is now for us something analogous to them, is no better than a self-contradiction. And it is this conclusion which after the requisite explanation (and even, as it may appear, with certain modifications) we must in the end undertake to defend.

The statement seems at first sight a paradox, and is open to every kind of external counter-assertion. To these or to some of these we must in the end return, but in the mean time we have to encounter a serious internal difficulty.

Our present point of view is as follows. A critical position towards history in general implies that the mass of historical material is no longer one with ourselves, is not any more carried about in and with us as a part of the substance which we feel to be natural to us, but has, as a possession, been separated from the mind, and is held apart from and over against it as an object which presents a problem for the intelligence. This object, although a possession, has not yet been appropriated; though we have it, yet we have not made it ours; and, though it is intrinsically rational, yet it has not been rationalized. We have seen further that, since all certainty with respect to the past depends ultimately upon present inference, the basis and foundation for the criticism of what has been, is necessarily formed by the knowledge of what is.

The difficulty which first meets us at this point presents itself in the following question. 'Is not that, which is to be the canon of testimony, itself dependent on testimony?' i.e. does not the present knowledge of the historian rest to a considerable extent on what others have told him, and in fact consist of this in no small degree? 'The historian,' it may be objected, 'does perhaps as critical divide the world of the past (as in the proper sense not yet known) from the present and known world; but the process is illusory, because this known world, which is the furniture of his mind, and the kosmos which forms the criterion for that which has not yet been systematized, is in itself largely built up of the communicated experience of others. Is it not then a flat contradiction to bring, as a canon, to criticism that which presupposes uncriticised testimony, and has absorbed it into all the the tissues of its organism?'

The objection demands consideration, but its force depends on our supposing that the present experience, which is to be taken as the historical canon, is mere common experience, and it is answered by the reflection that the testimony, which the present object involves, is, or at least ought to be, no uncriticised material. The experience in short which is to be the foundation of historical criticism must itself be a critical experience.

The object of critical experience can neither be said to be given, nor, so far as the individual critic is concerned, to grow. It is made (or it makes itself); it is a creation though not from nothing; it is the new-birth of an organism from matter organic but no longer in itself vital.

The contents, which in early life are taken into and build up our consciousness, consisting, as they do, of our individual experiences blended into one substance inextricably with the experiences of others, exist in the uncritical mind as that which (for itself at least) is a confused and unsystematized world of consciousness. It is to such a world that the critical intelligence awakens, and its awakening is the sundering of its material from itself. It stands (so far as awakened) a self-conscious unity on this side, and regarding its matter as from the outside demands from it the same oneness, that intelligible unity which, as the world of an intelligence, it is to have and virtually has. The new object, which now for the critical mind is the sole and increasing reality, is the re-organisation of the old world; it is true only because recreated, and can be recreated only because connected into a rational system. Every part here must live, and live in the life of the whole. The dead matter which was received on authority, and held true because it was so received, must render an account of its claims. It is true, if at all, now no longer as mere testimony, but because it has been examined, and satisfactorily mediated with the critical object as at present existing.

This is the condition of its re-vitalization, that it can be subsumed under the present critical world. But what then is this world, which thus in its hands has sentence of life and death? It is the world of critical observation. The ultimate real object, the final reference, and last basis is constituted by that which has been, or can be, personally verified in our own external or internal critical observation. If we are asked for the reason of our beliefs we are sooner or later in the last resort brought back to this; and it is thus our immediate personal (though that need not mean our individual) experience, on which, by many steps or by few, all our certainty depends.

Our answer then to the above objection is this. Certainly our present world contains matter of testimony, but not *as* matter of testimony. What we stand upon is personal observation; and what we have ground to connect with that we will receive because of its connection with that, and subject to appeal to that; and we will receive nothing else, but from that basis we will order our world.

But yet it is a matter of fact that our world is extended to fresh cases which (roughly speaking) have nothing analogous to previous phenomena. And, this being so, we are far at present from having established our contention that history is incapable of attesting to events without analogy in the present world. For why should not historical testimony furnish such non-analogous cases? Our answer must depend on the meaning we give to 'historical testimony.' *If* historical testimony implies more than probability, *if* it is equivalent to scientific evidence, then the above question remains unanswerable. There is no reason why such attestation should not be possible. But if we see cause (or choose) to oppose scientific to historical testimony, and to confine the latter to the sphere of the probable, then the question answers itself, so soon as we have discovered what are the conditions of the above extension to the non-analogous. What are these conditions?

That my real world can be widened by the taking in of new facts, and that apart from any special analogy, is indisputable. And in the first place (1) it may be so enlarged by my own observation. Let us take as an example the so-called 'mesmeric' phenomena. These may be said (with accuracy sufficient for the present purpose) to have possibly no analogy to anything in the observer's world hitherto; yet no one could maintain that it was impossible to know and to be certain of these phenomena as real facts. On the other hand no one would assert that these facts could be assured to us by the same amount of observation, as would be enough for phenomena of a class already recognized (wholly or partially), and capable of subsumption under an acknowledged head as a similar or subordinate case. In a word, if we are left to our own observation, and have nothing analogous to support us, we can indeed learn new facts with certainty, but on one condition only, namely that of the most careful examination often repeated.

So far direct observation. Let us pass now to testimony (2) and ask in the second place—Can I learn un-analogous facts mediately with equal certainty, and, if so, on what condition?

Let us take once more the 'mesmeric' phenomena. These may have no analogy in our own private experience; and yet we may receive the facts, on testimony, as no less certain than those which we find for ourselves. They are received, and that critically, as attested: but, on the other hand, (although not contrary to the conditions which make experience possible, nor yet in contradiction with the object he knows at present) they yet may be without any apparent analogy in the world of the individual critic.

Testimony rests on experience, and testimony goes beyond experience, and, as it would seem, without the support of experience. How is this possible? The answer is that in this, the strongest imaginable case, the testimony must be the strongest imaginable; it must be equal in validity to our own most careful observation. Nothing short of this is enough. The question then arises 'how is such validity possible, if, as we have seen, testimony must finally rest on an inference from personal knowledge, and if personal knowledge is ultimately based on our own intelligent observation?'

The explanation is this—that by inferences, however complicated yet in the end resting on personal observation, we have so apprehended and possessed ourselves of the consciousness of others, that we are justified in assuming the identity of their standpoint with our own; i.e. we can be assured that the already systematized world, which was brought as a canon by the witnesses to the observation and to the subsumption of the mesmeric phenomena, was practically the same as that which we ourselves should have brought. We thus are certain that the men can see for us, because we know that they are able to think for us. And, having this entire confidence, we run no risk beyond that which our own experience is at all times liable to, viz. the error arising from individual perturbation.

Or, in other words, by an inference from that which I know already I certainly discover that the witness's mind is an universe, a kosmos like my own and subject to the same laws; and hence, if I can conclude in addition to his integrity and his will to observe and judge, his judgment is to me precisely the same as my own. He may be right or wrong, but so may I; he is as likely to be right as I am; and I can only tell whether he is right by the same criteria which (apart from fresh observation) tell me that I am right. *If I am able to apply a negative and positive criticism to his new fact, as I do to my new fact, then his fact is as good as mine.* Our objective world is known to be the same, his subjective power of extending the object is known to be equal to mine, and the distinction of our individualities makes no difference to the matter itself.

We have seen that testimony, even without analogy, can be made part of our present critical object; but we have seen also on what condition. Testimony goes beyond individual experience, but not beyond *our* experience; or it takes us beyond our experience if it takes *us* with it. It is not uncriticised; it stands, if at all, on the basis of our world. It has been made subject to the laws of, and has been connected with and become part of, our personal experience, not in its own right *as* testimony, not in the right of the witness *as* witness, but in the right of and on the guarantee of our own intelligence.

The question proposed above 'Under what conditions is it possible to extend our experience to fresh phenomena, which (roughly speaking) are without analogy in what has been hitherto observed?' has been answered. Such enlargement, apart from our own observation, is possible only through the above described identification of consciousness. This is the one and the indispensable condition.

The bearing of the result will be seen more clearly, when exhibited in its negative form as an answer to the question, 'Under what conditions does testimony necessarily fail to establish a non-analogous case?' In the first place, we must say, wherever we are unable to verify the witness generally; in the second, wherever we cannot satisfy ourselves with respect to his particular procedure.

(1) In the first place wherever the standpoint of the witness differs (wholly or in relation to the particular class of facts in question) from our own, or wherever its agreement is not known to

us, there the testimony cannot stand without analogy from our own experience. For, however possible any matter may be, yet we cannot on testimony receive it as real, unless we have ground to connect it with the real. Analogy is such a ground, but, failing analogy, there is nothing left but the inference to a strength of testimony which can exist only on the assumption of the identification of our own with another's consciousness (in general, or in relation to one particular division of the world); and this assumption, in the case supposed at present, we have no right to make.

To repeat—Wherever the so-called 'fact' is made by subsumption under a view of the world different from ours, wherever we fail to make out that the judgment rested (consciously or unconsciously) on an ordered system identical with our own, there the 'fact' cannot be affirmed except on analogy; for, since the narrative is based on beliefs different from ours, the facts are affected by the beliefs, or, for anything we know, they may be so; we have no security that they are not affected. And the application of the above is, that any narrative of 'facts' which involves judgments proceeding from a religious consciousness or a view of the world, which, as a whole or in respect of the part in question, differs from ours, cannot have such force as to assure us of any event un-analogous to present experience.

(2) In the second place, even where we are able to be sure that the witness regarded his facts from a point of view identical with our own, yet, taking this for granted, wherever we are not able to assume the witness's integrity, and wherever we have not firm grounds for believing that the amount of careful and intelligent observation was brought to the case, which we ourselves should have considered necessary—there the identification of consciousness is still incomplete; the testimony is not equal to our own verification, and the matter of it must stand, if at all, on analogy, and apart from analogy cannot be received.

We have asked the question, Can our knowledge be extended by ourselves to embrace a fresh world of phenomena? and we have answered that question in the affirmative. We have stated the means, our own stringent observation. We have enquired again,

Can testimony similarly enlarge our experience, where analogy fails? and we have answered, Yes, where identification of consciousness is possible, but, where it is not possible, never. Never for this reason, that, to be critical, we must stand on our own experience, that an extended experience is ours when we make it, and that the matter of testimony, where it does not become ours in such a manner as to be valid of itself and directly, must be valid and ours indirectly by an inference from the basis of our present knowledge. Such conclusion is an analogy, and by a mere analogical argument you can not conclude to a non-analogous fact.

To this latter statement we shall have to return; but at present we have ended all that we have to say on testimony in general. We must pass to historical evidence in particular. We asserted above provisionally that in no case could historical testimony establish the non-analogous, that e.g. it could not attest the existence of 'mesmeric' phenomena. There seems at first sight no ground in the foregoing for such a contention. We must attempt however to justify it.

But such justification will be possible only at the cost of a considerable amount of assumption. What historical testimony can prove, and can not prove, must depend in the end upon what we mean by 'historical testimony.' The answer to this question we must take to no small degree for granted.

What is historical evidence? It seems, till we try it, so easy to say; but the effort assures us of the presence of difficulty.

When we speak of historical evidence, and when we emphasize the 'historical,' the accent is due to the contrast which, either disguisedly or openly, exists in our mind between 'scientific' and 'merely historical.' In general we imagine a distinction between the two sorts of testimony, but to put that difference into words is in any case arduous; and to do so, without the assumption of some point which is matter of controversy, is in the present state of opinion, I believe, impossible.

It is easy to bring forward a partial answer. We may say, if we will, that history is the testimony of the past to the past, while science is that of the present to the present, of the present in the sense of what *is* unchangeably: and this answer, if it is not the truth, must be said at any rate to have its truth. But for present purposes in its simple form it is altogether insufficient.

For in a certain sense we know *nothing* but the past. Scientific testimony, scientific observations are, like all things human, events in time, and while we grasp them as present they are gone. This is no psychological refinement: there is no one too sensible or too careless to apprehend at least that the present of to-day is the past of to-morrow, this week of next week, the last century of this century.

In a certain sense again we know nothing but the present. That the object of knowledge must be present is a truism; and historical evidence to be valid for us must be here and now before us.

And in practice the differences of time are of no more account than the differences in space. That a scientific experiment was made this year or last year may be in itself as utterly indifferent as the fact that it was made in England or America; the intervals are nothing to us. Historical testimony again may be what is called contemporary with ourselves; but in itself such a consideration does not necessarily lead us to belief or to disbelief. The orthodox Catholic of our day gets no hearing for his stories except from Catholics; and the tales of the uneducated concerning witchcraft or spectres do not find more favour from the fact that they belong to the present generation.

The distinction of past and present, as we see, will not help us from our puzzle; and our confusion is by no means lessened when we reflect that we can not name one single event which, in certain quarters, would not be considered an object for science—'science' to be construed in the narrow meaning of physical science, and the event to be taken in the unlimited extent of its entire signification. On the other hand the reflection meets us, that, in the opinion of many, there is not one single 'scientific' fact which, as an event, can be excluded from history, if we allow ourselves the fullest use of the word.

In view of such complications, when we find that the objects attested to by history and science are apparently indistinguishable, and that the date of the attesters matters nothing in itself, we are at a loss to perceive any longer that distinction in kind we imagined to exist.

If further we confine this distinction to degree, and say history with its evidence is probable, while certainty belongs to the essence of science, we perhaps shall have stated what is altogether true, and in words at least shall have established our contention. For if history as a whole be probable, and if every probable detail be admitted to rest on an argument from analogy, then that the matter of historical testimony stands, if at all, on an analogical argument is an obvious conclusion. But it is in words alone that the assertion is made good, while the difference to be made manifest is simply obscured. We shall be found merely to have asserted that everything which is certain is matter of science, and that everything not provable is matter of history.

To identify the matter of science and history is not only in itself a serious assumption where the meaning of science is *natural* science; but it also for our purpose is practically useless. It is useless, because the terms 'scientific' and 'historical' will not help us in the least towards a result, but in this sense will merely express the result itself. They will be empty synonyms for 'certain' or 'probable.'

It is not worth while to linger over efforts at definition like the above. The attempts are hopeless. To maintain the distinction at all the sphere of history must be limited; and history can be limited only in the face of counter-propositions. To define historical testimony we must divide the whole which some think indivisible, and to do this by proof involves an engagement along the whole front of the position.

For our purpose here there is nothing practicable except to assume what we think is necessary, and to remember that it remains an assumption throughout.

We take historical testimony in the first place (1) to be *in* history, i.e. we confine it within the field of *human tradition*. Geological, geographical evidence, evidence from excavations, and evidence from language, we refuse to consider as properly historical. The reason is this, that they do not essentially lie within the period of human records; and history-writing is to count for us here as the limit of critical history.

Historical testimony in the second place (2) is *to* history. Astronomical or meteorological records, the whole account kept of natural events, are, as we understand it, not part of history. History for us too is a record of events, but the record of a single field, the tradition and the tale of the deeds and sufferings of *men*.

The theory which science may construct of the developement of our system or of the planet on which we live; the story of the origin of animal life and the growth of its varied species, the account of the generation of humanity itself with its early stages and slow gradations—these we may accept (as we all do and must accept them) in some sense or other; but they one and all for our present enquiry must fall beyond the historical limit. Such evidence it not historical evidence.

We must go still farther. The records of the science of the day to its present human phenomena; the observations and experiments recorded by the physiologist or doctor, and even the narrations of empirical psychology—these in addition we refuse (so far as scientific) to consider under the head of historical testimony. Historical *material* they may be. (Is there anything human which may not be?) There is no human record which is not historical material, and therefore in a sense historical testimony also. It is not however the facts as attested which in such a case fall within the field of history. It is not the facts which are historical, but only the fact of their attestation, which latter belongs to a different world. To express the same thing more simply, scientific evidence is a human phenomenon which in itself is not scientific.

What is the ground of our refusal above? The following—Not only must historical testimony be in history and to history, but it also (3) must have its origin in an historical interest.

The interest of science is the discovery of the laws of what *is*, neither past nor present nor future events, nor events at all, but only the abiding. The interest of history is in the recalling of a course of events which *are not*, which neither exist nor will exist, but which *have* existed. The object of the one is 'the permanent amid change,' the object of the other 'the changes of the perma-

nent;' facts to the one are illustrations, to the other are embodi-
ments; the individuals of the one are limited to be abstracted, of the
other are incorporated to be realized.

In more simple language, the interest at the basis of scientific
testimony is to use the particular case just so far as to get the
universal *out of it;* the concretion of life is worth having solely for
the sake of the abstract relations it contains. But the interest
which gives birth to historical testimony is a human interest, an
interest in the particular realization. Our common nature, which is
personal in us all, feels in each one of us 'that nothing human is
alien to ourselves.' Our interest in the past is our feeling of oneness
with it, is our interest in our own progression; and because this
human nature to exist must be individual, the object of historical
record is the world of human individuality, and the course of its
developement in time. For scientific testimony the man is a mere
example, for historical never: he is a new incarnation of the same
felt substance, the manifest individualization, it may be, at highest,
of a stage in progress (but on this point we wish to express no
opinion.) For the universal *as such* the historical witness cares not
at all; at most it concerns him to see it embodied in a single person
or the spirit of a nation.

It is possible, we admit, that where matters are so complex, and
the tendencies of the mind so mix and meet, that the testimony of
science may wander for the time to a merely historical field and
interest; it is possible again that a record made for purposes of
science may cover in addition the ground of history. In the first
case the testimony is merely historical and not scientific; in the
second case the testimony is both. It is primarily scientific and
incidentally historical; it is more than historical, and in considering
historical testimony we must be allowed to exclude it from our
conclusion.

But in the vast majority of cases the three conditions we have
just explained will be found sufficient to distinguish the testimony
of history and of science. Doubtful cases will remain and must
remain. The story of the plague at Athens might well have been
told either from the point of view of history or from that of science;
as it stands perhaps it belongs to both. The field of 'mesmeric' and

similar phenomena, in the sphere between physiology and psychology, would afford a variety of evidence, passing by slow degrees from the scientific to the historical, and from thence to a region which holds of neither science nor history. But these cases do not trouble our general distinction. Our rule must be this; we must first discover, as we can, whether the testimony is to be called historical or not: in the second place we must ask whether, being historical, it is at the same time more, whether it is also scientific. This second class which is also scientific (i.e. such evidence as would be allowed to constitute the proof or part of the proof of a scientific generalization) we do not call simple historical testimony, and wherever it exists the following conclusions have no application.

We have narrowed 'historical testimony' to a limited field; and we have been forced to renounce the smallest attempt to justify our procedure. Arbitrary as that may appear it is not so altogether; and the result will I think accord with the beliefs of the majority.

Having attempted in some measure to define our terms we can take up the question once more, 'Is historical testimony capable of extension to the non-analogous?'

We can now put that question in its other form, 'Is historical evidence probability or proof?' Into this general distinction it is impossible here to enter. It must be taken for granted, and wherever it is not allowed, wherever fact and probability are identified, there we admit the conclusions of this essay are without validity.

Is the matter of history probable or certain? We believe it to be probable; but this does not mean that about all its contents there is practically a doubt. It means that, be there never so many converging lines of probable reasoning, yet these never transcend the region of practical certainty. The result is never theoretically proved.

An historical 'proof' may be conclusive, in so far that we can not doubt; a legal 'proof' may in many cases leave room for no possible hesitation; but neither the one nor the other is for us a scientific demonstration.

The matter of historical testimony is, we believe, not a certainty but a probability. The grounds of this assertion will be given below; but let us in the first place (1) suppose that it is admitted to be probable; then the conclusion will follow that it can not extend to events without analogy in the sphere of present certainty.

Why is this? It is because in history we have a probable conclusion, which at the same time is required to stand as certain; an hypothesis which cannot be scientifically verified, but which nevertheless is to be taken as a fact; and the only means, the sole justification of such a result is in the accordance of the conclusion of the hypothesis with the known world. And that is the present world, the verifiable world, the world of to-day, or (in another application of the term) the world of science.

The propositions of science cannot be probable; the scientifically probable is not yet scientific doctrine. The theories of historical fact again are not probable in the sense that they are simply the statement of open questions. They are results; and where no result is possible, no history exists. But, resting on mere probable evidence, to come to a result beyond the limit of analogy, when we know in the present world no similar ·case, nor any tendency which makes in the direction—this is the procedure, we think, of no reasonable person.

And it should not be forgotten that, if the interest of history is not the enlargement of the territory of science, but rather the exhibition of the oneness of humanity in all its stages and under all its varieties, if it is ourselves that we seek in the perished (and is there anything else which we can seek?)—if the object of our endeavour is to breathe the life of the present into the death of the past, and re-collect into this pantheon of the mind the temporal existences which once seemed mortal, then, where we encounter an alien element, which we cannot recognise as akin to ourselves, that interest fails, the hope and the purpose which inspired us dies, and the endeavour is thwarted. The remembrance of our childhood and our youth is the sweetest of pleasures, for it gives us the feeling of ourselves, as the self of ourself and yet as another; and the failure to recognise, or the impossibility of interest in our earlier life, is, to those whom it has befallen, the bitterest pain of the most cruel estrangement.

But to resume——If historical conclusions are probable, they are subject to analogy.* Next we must ask if they ever are more than probable ?

This question (2) we answer in the negative. If more than probable they must needs be scientific; they would be equal to the results of our critical observation, and for this, as we have seen, is required both identification of standpoint, and assurance of sufficient integrity and carefulness.

To these the nature of historical testimony presents insurmountable obstacles.

In the first place (A) we must remember that historical testimony not only is *to* history, but is also *in* history. This addition prevents the identification of our minds with the minds of the witnesses. For history (i.) (we assume it) is progressive, is a progress not only in the sense of that which increases in quantity, but in the sense of that which developes or evolves itself, is essentially the same in stages of growth which are diverse in quality, which differ from each other even more than the blossom from the bud, and the fruit from the blossom.

If the bud were self-conscious it would know of itself, but not in the way that the blossom knows it, still less as the fruit knows it : and as failing of the truth its knowledge must be said to be false.†

Still more is it so with history. In that ceaseless process which differentiates itself only as a means to integration, and which integrates itself only with the result of a fuller differentiation, the consciousness of the earlier stage of humanity is never the consciousness of a later developement. The knowledge it has of itself is partial and false when compared with the epoch of an intenser realization. And when we reflect that for this highest developement it is that history exists, we see that it is a hope doomed only to disappointment, when the present expects in the mind of the past to find the views and beliefs of the present.

If the stages of evolution were essentially diverse, the possibility of history is inconceivable; and if history were a manifestation of human phenomena where all but the accidental was simply the

---

* See on this point Appendix, Note C. † This illustration is borrowed.

same, the interest it excites would in no respect be higher than the pleasure we take in an ordinary novel.

To proceed——Not only is man's nature progressive, but (ii.) history is concerned, so to speak, with the most human part of humanity, and hence the most fully progressive. The conscious deeds and sufferings, the instinctive productions, and unconscious destinies of men and of nations live most with the special and characteristic life of an individual epoch; and it is the time, and the children of the particular time which alone are the past for which history cares.

And not only is the matter of history in progress, not only again does history select that element which progress affects the most, but thirdly (iii.) within that sphere its interest leads it to the most distinctive embodiment of the passing stage; not to those social relations which possess a limited permanence, but to the striking, the temporal, in a word the individual.

And as is the interest so is the subject interested. The historical witness is also the son of his time, and, in relation to that which bears most the stamp of the era, his mind is the reflection of the age in a mirror which shares its nature. It is thus that, in his character of recorder, his point of view, when he relates phenomena dissimilar to ours, will also itself not fail to be dissimilar.

For science it is true the observations of the one age are valid for the conclusions of another; and that, it may be added, where no present analogy is perhaps in existence. The facts of 'mesmerism' could be proved, we doubt not, by simple scientific testimony; and astronomical observations are accepted as facts, and doubtless would be so no less, in case they were supported by no analogy. The reason of this is, of course, that we are able so to reconstruct the observers and the conditions of their observations, as to possess ourselves entirely of their faculties, and use them as our own. And the possibility of this consists in the fact that science abstracts. It takes account not of all phenomena, but in each of its divisions of a separate and limited province, and it uses, so to speak, not the whole but a part alone of the observer's consciousness.

The object of science does not transform itself in a ceaseless progress, and the subject of science can separate itself from the concrete developement of the historical mind, and can remain practically identical while coexisting with standpoints generally diverse. But this with history is impossible.

Not only do we fail to possess ourselves of the historical witness in such manner as to secure scientific proof, but secondly (B), were this even the case, to reconstruct the particular observation is well nigh impossible.

For the original fact of history is (i.) an event which perishes as it arises. It dies and it can never be recalled. It cannot repeat itself, and we are powerless to repeat it. And in addition (ii.) we can not prepare for it.

We may be ignorant of its approach; and if we were aware of that, yet to post ourselves in the fitting locality may be out of our power; or, given our presence at the time and place, still the fact is too complex for a certain observation. To fix you must isolate; and how can you isolate here?

And, given your power to isolate and to fix, yet too often you know not the important point. The moment which decides the movement of a complication reveals itself as such when the tendency is established; and then from our knowledge of the present too late we deplore our ignorance in the past.

And further there remains (iii.) yet another consideration, which weakens still further (as compared with juridicial) well-nigh the whole of historical testimony. With the possible exception of contemporary evidence the historian is unable to cross-examine his witnesses. He can, by a critical analysis of the deposition, as a whole in relation to its parts, and of the relations which the parts bear to one another, and further by a comparison with other statements, to a certain extent make good this defect. But his procedure remains in the end but a wretched substitute, and a permanent source of weakness.

Such are the obstacles in the way of a scientific historical proof. The result of their consideration is this—that, even in case the historian should succeed in exhibiting identity of standpoint, yet the further reconstruction will never be complete enough to take him beyond a mere probability; and hence, since a probable conclusion must rest on analogy, that therefore the non-analogous is excluded for ever from the sphere of historical testimony.

This result we believe to be simply the theoretical expression of the best historical practice; and when there is one single supposed event in tradition, to which present experience can supply no analogy, which yet remains unchallenged by criticism, then and not till then will it be necessary to ask how such a condition of things can exist, and to attempt to reconcile with it the doctrine we have now put forward and endeavoured to defend.

This doctrine is at all events the reverse of sceptical. The present experience, which is open to our research, is so wide in its extent, is so infinitely rich in its manifold details, that to expect an event in the past to which nothing analogous now corresponds may fairly be considered a mere extravagance. And taking again historical testimony, as we have it now, there will be few, I think, who on reflection will find the above conclusions either forced on the facts or strained beyond them; or whose point of view will render impossible their general adoption.

But it will be urged that existing historical witnesses are no fair sample of historical testimony, that what may be or is does not mean what ought to be, and that first the conclusion has been fixed, and then a term has been narrowed to suit it. This in any case has not been done; but it is perfectly true that, if historical testimony be used in a more extensive sense, the above conclusion fails to apply.

History perhaps is a science to generalize what is, to discover the laws of phenomena. If it is this, then historical evidence not only may be but must be scientific; and nothing but scientific testimony has a right to be called historical. But in a world where all that we find in existence is so hard to understand, it seems idle to reflect on what merely is to be; and to speculate on a mere discounted possibility (or perhaps impossibility) is never, I think, a legitimate proceeding.

Let us suppose though that history is really to be a science, and one thing is clear from the first, that the mass of existing historical testimony is non-scientific, and well-nigh (if not altogether) devoid of the smallest value. The necessary scientific evidence must be made.

'It is being made' (we shall be told of course) 'and that by statistics:' but to see the relations which the elements of particular societies bear to one another, or even to generalize laws, which apparently in all societies are likely to be more or less correct, is one thing. It is one thing to discover permanent relations in the stationary; and, if history were stationary (if we could say of it that it was and is to eternity) in that case the science of history would be a far simpler expectation.

But it is another, an altogether and an utterly different undertaking, to find the eternal laws which 'explain' the changes of an unending evolution, which is for us only so far as it has made itself, and each stage of which is the qualitative new-birth of an organic, and more than an organic, unity, which resumes its lower developements in a fresh integration, and informs its elements with its own distinctive nature. If the 'explanation' of the developement of a man's individuality in every case presupposes the result it arrives at, and 'explains' in the end nothing that is individual—then it must be a more futile attempt for us who have not the result before us, mere children who have seen and known no more than the childhood of humanity, to 'explain' from that the future of its life, and to reach the laws which will evolve its character, through successive individualizations, from youth to manhood and from manhood to age. In this way to seize the 'red strand of necessity' in progress is surely impossible, and 'science of tendencies' is an amiable phrase, which sounds not much better than 'science of intentions.'

And, if this science of progress is to be possible in itself, yet, where everything turns on recording, as they arise, the essential facts, there presents itself at once a new impediment. The essential facts are the determining element of movement, and the means to a fresh end; but to apprehend the means implies the knowledge of the end, to know the essential movement involves the knowledge of the terminus. But, confined as we are to a limited stage, with the heights above us hidden from our eyes, (what we *are*, that we know), there remains to us nothing but either to secure the whole of the events, and this is impossible; or to run in imminent danger of recording those facts which are not essential, and hence are useless for the science of progress. It is a common-place that the past has recorded too much that we could well spare, and too little of that we would most gladly know. Will it not be so always? What we think the important phenomena of 1870 and '71 may perhaps have eluded our accurate observation, and in 1971 may with other things be a matter of controversy, while as for the interest of the historian of 1971, and the facts which bear most in his mind on progress, of these perhaps we have simply no notion.

So much in passing—but if after all there can really exist historical testimony which is more than probable, it must fall outside of and destroy our conclusion; and of course can assure us of non-analogous facts, since it is of such strength as to be valid evidence for a law of science.

We have ended the first, and by far the largest, division of our subject. We have found the principle of critical history, and have now to see its application to existing testimony. But let us briefly resume our present result.

We have seen so far that history is matter of inference; that every inference rests on a presupposition; and that this presupposition is formed by present experience. We have further shown that, although this experience is not always personal in the sense of that which we can immediately verify for ourselves, it yet is personal in the sense that upon the observation and judgment of our own mind it ultimately depends. We have shown that it is present, not in the sense of connection with this or that moment, but in the sense of belonging to no moment in particular. We have shown that this character belongs alone to scientific testimony, that the material of history must hence be subject to analogy; and this distinction we have endeavoured to strengthen and defend.

Criticism is now left fronting the material to recreate which it possesses and feels both the mission and the strength. And this may be considered an artificial position, in so far as the individual critic never does actually separate himself from the whole of his historical knowledge, but invariably brings with him to the work a portion of the traditional object, already rationalized and made part of his present and critical world. Nor is this apparent anticipation of his result unjustified in the individual, if that, which he brings as a canon to criticism, has been itself already confronted with criticism, and rationalized by virtue of it—i.e. has been concluded to be actual fact from a critical standpoint, which is essentially the same as the critic's own. For the true world is continually growing, and when part of history has been made real, it at once becomes a means for the realization of the remainder. Artificial then as the complete separation of criticism from its material appears and moreover is, when we regard the individual alone, yet it is far from being so as soon as we consider the process of criticism in itself.

History, in the character of historical criticism, views its contents as lying outside itself, and its task is once more to contain them within itself. But to this the very nature of the contents presents an obstacle. The contents are records, which in a twofold manner claim to be received as real facts; first as the record of some particular age and author, and secondly in the character of recorded events. If now the whole mass were found to be completely mediated, subject to the conditions, and according to the analogy of present experience; if namely the events narrated were consistent, were possible, and followed in a sequence, of which the causes and the results were in some measure known to us; and if further the dates, and the general credibility of the writers were established by a satisfactory train of inference—in that case criticism would have no task before it, save the work of verifying and re-affirming under its own guarantee the unchanged material in its original shape.

But how far, how entirely such a supposed state of things is removed from reality, needs not to be remarked. It does not exist, and the mode in which the matter of history is produced does not admit of its possible existence. It would indeed be strange if every record were authentic and trustworthy, if the judgments of a succession of witnesses scattered along the developement of human progress were all secured from error, and without alteration could be harmonized into one connected whole. No one at the present time would dare to say that such is the case; and, if such is not the case, then criticism, if it is to be criticism, must necessarily be to a certain extent negative.

So much is generally seen, but there is something more which cannot be said to be seen and generally admitted, namely this—that a negative criterion, if it exist at all, must be from its nature an absolute criterion, or be a self-contradiction. To the consciousness which never has risen to the critical point of view, 'facts are stubborn things,' and the most stubborn of all are those which the mind feels it has no share in, and which come to it with the weight of external authority. We have seen however what these facts are made of, and, at the point we have reached, it needs no lengthy reflection to justify the negative character of criticism.

Criticism from its very essence can not be simply affirmative. The object which is to be criticized has ceased to be the real object, since for criticism it is the critical and that alone which is the real, and the uncritical object is consequently negated in its old, and not yet re-affirmed in its new character. Criticism, if it be criticism, must in the beginning and provisionally suspect the reality of every thing before it; and if there are some matters which it can not re-affirm without falsifying itself, these matters have themselves to thank. If indeed it is so that this is their lot, that they cannot withdraw from criticism because in their very substance is involved and admitted that principle which in criticism becomes conscious of itself, and if yet to submit to criticism be for them to be transmuted or to be destroyed—this is no charge to lay against the arbitrariness of the critic. It is the contradiction implicit in the facts which to their own destruction has become explicit, and if they are denied it is only because they deny themselves.

If for history the fact means that which is real, and if the real means that which criticism has affirmed, it should not be forgotten that it is mere nonsense to talk of anything as 'an historical fact' unless criticism has been able to guarantee it as such.

There may be professed historical events, which in themselves, since they are represented without historical antecedent or sequent, contradict the conception of an historical fact (are the opposite of that which an event must be in order to exist for history) and, as they stand, history cannot even discuss their possibility.

There may be events which, though in themselves coming under the conditions of history, can yet be supported by no analogy from present experience, and, despite their testimony, they must wait for farther experience.* There may be events which, though both possible and analogous, are mediated with the real by no sufficient connection, and until connected they are not yet rationalized. And lastly there are narrated facts which criticism can reaffirm as certain or probable. We must ask ourselves in what this process consists.

The historical material, as has been before stated, is twofold and presents to criticism two sides, on the one side the author, on the other the events recorded. Criticism must attempt on the one side to identify its consciousness, so far as possible, with that of the writer, by inference to establish his power and his will to narrate faithfully; on the other to find in the events recorded laws analogous to those which have been observed in present experience and in history so far as already rationalized. If the task be fully accomplished the facts are historically certain, if partially they are considered probable; but in each case they retain their original shape.

But these events thus reasserted by criticism form no continuous whole, the series presents gaps which a positive process is necessary to fill, and the process is an inferential recreation according to law from a basis of present experience or of the historical certainty already attained. It is a sufficient answer to any difficulties which may be raised as to the construction of a past order to point to the procedure of our police courts, where, in addition to the reconstruction of the witnesses by cross-examination, the sequence of events is reached by an active combination from present data. The inadequacy however of the historical material both in respect of quantity and quality makes the completion in this manner of the series of events an impossibility, and the persistent attempts to join the open links by the creation of causes and motives can lead to nothing but an overstrained Pragmatism, which fills the past with those fancies and opinions which only belong to the individual consciousness of the writer.

Thus far criticism has given an account of that portion only of its material which has been able to be realized because found to be already rational. There is still a remainder which has not been rationalized, which in other language because incapable of forming

* See Appendix, Note D.

in its own shape a part of the true object, must be considered as simply subjective.

Error is here presupposed, and the task of criticism is, by the removal of error, where possible to restore the truth. The process, as before, admits of a twofold method, namely the reconstruction of the supposed historical fact either from its inward or outward side, by inference on the one side from the mental character of the witness or on the other side from the course of events, and where the operation is successful the fact once more takes its place in the world of reality, still as an outward event but new-begotten and transformed.

It may be no unwarrantable digression to call attention once more to the view which in different forms we have so often encountered, according to which here the removal of mistake by criticism has for its result the 'original fact.' But in the present case the 'original fact' is primarily for history a fallacious inference, and if by the 'original fact' be meant again that which the fact should have been, still this for history is an inference, the theory of a theory, whose result is a double-distilled theory.

There is still an unrationalized material remaining for history as a problem, alleged outward events which can be taken into the real series neither as unchanged nor yet as transmuted into other outward events. But even in this case criticism is not powerless; for, although the mistaken outward fact can not be resolved into the real outward fact, we may none the less deal with the mistake itself, and the exhibition of those conditions which caused the wrong assertion of an outward fact is for criticism the satisfactory mediation of the alleged fact as a link in the historical sequence: the outward has now an existence, real indeed but inward, and assured to us only so far as inward.

These are the processes of criticism by which it makes its own the alienated material of tradition, whether in the form of outward occurrences or in that of inward events; but there must ever remain elements which it can not reappropriate, and in many cases the testimony must be taken simply as testimony, the existence of which is historical, but the real fact, or, in other words, the explanation of which can not be given because we do not possess the data for its reconstruction.

The fact as attested may be possible, and in this case we lack the inference necessary to make it, as attested, part of history; or the attested fact may be historically impossible, and in this case we know that, as attested, it can never be part of history.

In neither of these cases can the testimony be explained as arising from the real existence of the attested. But it will be objected that we are bound to account for the testimony otherwise, or else accept the supposed fact. 'Testimony is a phenomenon,' says Paley, 'and the truth of the fact solves the phenomenon.' 'Testimony is a phenomenon;' that is indisputable, and as testimony it has its place in history; 'the truth of the fact solves the phenomenon;' that is equally certain, and we could wish that we had any means of knowing the solution. 'But,' we shall be answered, 'it is the assumption of the existence of the attested fact which is this solution.' That however depends entirely upon the nature of the fact alleged. The phenomenon to be solved is an historical phenomenon, and its solution must be an historical solution, and to propose as this solution a fact which, when taken as historical, contradicts the very notion of history, and dissolves together with history both itself and every other certain event, this is a proposition which may indeed do credit to its author's zeal, but hardly to his prudence.

But if we are unable to accept the averred fact because it is either as yet without guarantee, or because it is an historical impossibility, are we then bound to account otherwise for the phenomenon of the testimony? Can it be urged against us that our theory contains within itself facts which contradict it, and that we must solve the facts or abandon the theory? By no means, for this is to confound that which is negatively with that which is positively irrational. These unrationalized recorded events are in contradiction with criticism only when affirmed by criticism, but now, in the character of objects which history does not yet know, they are nothing positive; they fall as yet without the theory; they are no foreign body taken up within the system, but are as yet an external and unassimilated crudity. The reproach, if such it be, that for history without the known there lies a still unknown, without the real a still unrealized, is a reproach not hard for history to bear, since she bears it in common with the whole of human knowledge.

No! it is no disgrace to be ignorant where the problem is recognized and the effort is made. And it may be that those who in some particular field have made that effort, and made it not in vain, may yet by trial and failure have learnt to regard perhaps one phenomenon, or it may be more,* as incapable of resolution. This for the individual may be inevitable, but absolutely to assert the insolubility of any one historical element is to give offence to the consciousness of criticism and to strengthen the cause of her enemies. Historically to *account* for a phenomenon may not always be possible ; but it

---

* I had in my mind here the two passages in Baur's *Kirchengeschichte* (B. i. ss. 39-40, and again 45), where he has expressed himself in a somewhat unsatisfactory manner. There are two points to be kept clear. (i.) That Baur intended to exclude from the field of criticism *any historical event*, is, I think, quite out of the question. That which 'lies without the sphere of historical investigation' is, he means to imply, not an event, not a fact for critical history at all : though it may be an object for a higher form of knowledge. Secondly (ii.) when in both cases the spiritual process, which to Baur is the sole historical fact, is declared to be impenetrable by analysis, surely in this there is nothing to call for any great amount of surprise. What Baur may very well have meant is that there are results for which no 'genetic developement' will account, or give a reason, however much it may 'explain' them ; and processes again (as we see, for example, in the case of many works of art) the elements of which defy distinction, because indissolubly fused within particular personalities by a flame, which mixes the substance of the elements with the nature of the vessel that holds them, and which itself is the new-birth of an individual soul. Hence they are not natural growths but creations ; and if we like to call them miracles, we may. Sooner that, I conclude Baur would have added, than 'world-historical humbugs ;' since the supposed reality of this latter phrase, however much it may (or may not) explain, will certainly account for nothing, and itself can not be accounted for. It is a standing contradiction, a barbarous sideroxylon. If this is all that Baur had in his mind, it certainly involves no antagonism to critical history, but passes into a higher region. Concerning this region however it is altogether beyond our scope to say anything. Still Baur expressed himself in such a way as to make misunderstanding to the full as possible as understanding : and he was misunderstood. Strauss' criticism (as it appears in the translation of his second 'Life,' vol. i. p. 398) seems to me to rest on a misapprehension of point (i.) As to point (ii.) Holsten (see the two first divisions of his 'Zum Evangelium des Paulus und des Petrus') has attempted in a striking manner the analyses Baur pronounced impossible. I think however that it is a serious mistake to imagine that by the success or failure of such attempts the *principle* of criticism is in any way affected. These remarks have become perhaps too long : my excuse must be that the man whose procedure they discuss is worthy of this and more, if it were only worthy of him.

behoves us always to attempt to exhibit its historical origin as the result of known historical conditions; and in this sense its *possible* 'explanation' must be considered in every case as beyond a doubt. Every phenomenon has a possible solution, because as historical it must be the result of an historical antecedent; and the cause is a possible object of knowledge because the result is known already as that which by its very nature is a member in a series of links, the essence of which is to be knowable. Historical events there may be which are destined to remain for us always problems, but problems they remain for us and ever will remain, and their absolute insolubility, if we rightly consider it, involves no less than a contradiction in terms.

We have reached the end set before us, and the title 'Presuppositions of Critical History' is, I hope, in some measure explained and justified. To have set in the presuppositions of history generally (or of history viewed as a whole) a larger task before me was once my wish. It was a desire too serious for accomplishment by me, but the truth of what has been done at present is perhaps, so far as it goes, independent of a wider result. For however humble the sphere of her rule, yet at least, while within that sphere, criticism is subject to no intrusion and oppressed by no authority. She moves on her path unheedful of the warning, unheedful of the clamour of that which beyond her realm may be or may call itself religion and philosophy: her philosophy and her religion are the realization and the fruition of herself, and her faith is this, that while true to herself she can never find an enemy in the truth.

APPENDIX.

‑‑‑‑‑‑‑‑‑‑

NOTE A.

If we wish to see with our eyes the material and the task of the historian, we must imagine a fresco representing in a continual progress the figures and the actions of generations. And this is not the work of a single artist. On the contrary the artists are many with the many generations, and at times there is more than one in a single division of the picture. But though they are many they are not all painters from the life; for some lived after the time when the figures they pourtrayed had perished. And of these latter some with their names have told us that they borrowed from copies now lost, and of others we do not know even this; while of some again we can see that they copied, and copied wrongly, from original drawings which we still have.

So the fresco is not simple, nor by any means one work; but in certain parts of it, representative of certain ages, we have many diverse pictures of the same figure, which all profess to be copied from the life; and over other spaces of several generations there are no drawings at all which profess to be original, but instead of them the painting of an artist of after years, who had only, if we believe the best that we can, the sketches of others to work from. And in some cases there may be one such secondary artist, but over other spaces there may be two, or three, or more; and these may not agree with one another.

Nor is this all—we have not only the differences of diverse primary painters in some spaces, and in other spaces the discrepancies of secondary artists, but in process of time the later painters have agreed in this, that the picture must be a copy of the reality, but as to the reality they have disagreed, all with the picture as it was before them, and each with one another. And wishing to have a copy of the original they have all corrected the old figures or confusions of figures, and have remodelled and altered them to what they thought must be the life.

And the corrections of these artists have been themselves corrected by others who lived at the same time or after, so that at the first sight and to the careless eye the alterations only are to be seen, and not the underlying material. However to the man who examines and searches, the whole chaos is visible, the drawings which call themselves original, the representations where there are no such drawings, and then, on and over these, the ceaseless corrections and re-corrections, combinations and re-combinations of later artists.

But this mass is the picture, and the picture represents the original. So says the world, the present generation; but it adds, 'We cannot see the original, and the artist must make us a painting which will show us the men and the times as they were. The present picture is certainly a copy of the real persons; as they were so have they been drawn; we will not have them altered, but we must see them. Make a picture out of them!'

Is this sense or nonsense? The new picture is to be a copy of the reality, or else it is to be no picture; and the reality does not exist, and so can not be copied. 'Who thought of copying it?' will be the answer. 'We *have* the copy in the fresco.' Then why send for an artist when you only want a photograph? Or, rather, why copy at all? If you have one copy, which is already before you, what interest can you possibly have in reproducing that? 'But the artist is not merely to reproduce. Of course he is not to alter, much less to invent, but he must put the scattered materials together.' If however he copies every diverse representation, and encloses the collection in a single frame, whether it agree together or whether it do not—let him quote what precedent he may, he shall not prevent our asking, *Is* this a picture? A picture represents the real, and the real is one and is self-consistent; but here the figures of the real are many and are inconsistent, and only the frame is one.

'You have not understood us. The artist is to make a picture *out of* the fresco; and *because* the reality is one *therefore* the picture will be one, and so will answer to the real.' But the real is known only through the picture, and the picture is not one nor self-consistent. If you know that the truth in itself is one, you know it apart from the picture and in spite of the picture, and you know what the truth is, *that* the picture is not. *How* do you know that as it stands the picture can not be a copy of the real? Because you know *both* original *and* copy, and you compare the two together.

'That is part true and part false,' will be the reply. 'It is absurd to think we know anything of the past apart from the fresco, for this reason, that the real can not be invented but only copied, and the past is so perished that all that we have is the copy of it. But of course we know that what is real must be self-consistent because we can see that everywhere.'

Except in the fresco. 'Yes! but that is because the different sides and parts are so scattered; bring them together, and they will represent the real, and still be a copy.

This is the imagined task of the artist. He is not to know the original except from the fresco; and yet he is to know that the original is homogeneous, while the fresco is heterogeneous. And this is not a consistent theory. But let us pass to practice: let us see the painter at work.

He finds that in many places his materials are in a state of the completest contradiction. He finds perhaps that A kills B and marries his wife, and that B kills A and marries his wife, and then he comes to the corrections, or the 'harmonies,' or the rationalizations of later artists, some of whom represent both courses of events together, while most recombine or correct or simplify.

The artist has his orders. He is to make one picture or series of pictures, and he must not alter. He of course in fact both must and does alter; but let us suppose that he abides by his instructions; then he does nothing, or rather he returns to his patrons, and informs them that their task is a sheer impossibility.

And so they are driven to reflection, and they see perhaps that it is because the fresco is *not* a copy of the real, that the need for a picture has been felt; and it may be they assent at length to the alteration of the material. But they do not ask themselves the question, 'Is a picture a copy?' and they do not enquire, 'How is the supposed reality of the false copy to be denied at all, if we do not know the original?'

With their denial of the knowledge of the original they combine their assertion that the picture is a false copy of that original; and the result of their reflection is this, that the copy is a false copy because it is not a *mere* copy; and it is not a mere copy because it has not been *copied*, because it has not been taken from the life but altered and reconstructed.

But how are we to know what is a copy? 'There is no difficulty; we know that if we know that it has been copied.' And how in the world are we to tell this? 'We are sure of it because the drawings are contemporary.' Yet surely the *professedly* original drawings do not cover the whole space of the fresco, and even of these we find on examination that some are in a style which belongs to a later age, and in these cases we doubt the genuineness of the signatures. Are these copies too?

No not these, if you can show there are such, but the drawings of eye-witnesses reproduce the reality.

This seems at first sight something more tangible; but in practice we are still assailed by difficulties. In the first place the professed original drawings leave great gaps in the space of the fresco; in the second we have in every case to determine whether the drawing is really contemporary and genuine, and for this at present we have no criterion; and in the third place we find drawings, which have to be taken all alike as copies of the reality, in irreconcilable hostility to one another.

We return baffled for further instructions. 'Of course,' we are admonished, 'it is not enough that the painter has been contemporary: he must also be willing and he must be able to copy accurately, and his relative value is to be found by study and examination.'

But by study of what? Of the fresco, or anything beside the fresco?

'Certainly you must not confine your attention to the fresco. There is painting going on all around you. You can see what are the signs of an honest copyist and an able copyist. You must apply these to the drawings in the fresco, and so will reach the reality by discovering where the artists have strayed from the right style. And as to the genuineness of the work, you ought by observation to know the marks of the truthful copyist, and the marks of the inventor and fabricator.'

Then it is not enough that the painter should be honest?

'No, for he can be clumsy; and so two honest painters can produce two contradictory copies. He must be able as well, and you must judge of this by the character of his work. If he is honest and able his work will be truthful and natural.'

But it is time to recall the original position of the artist's employers, and place it by the side of their present instructions. At first the figures of the fresco were to be reproduced without questioning or alteration, whereas now before reproduction we are to ask Is this true? Is this natural? Have we a correct copy on the side of the artist? Have we a genuine fact for him to copy? And we find that we cannot ask ourselves these questions, till we know what is meant by a natural figure, and what is a faithful drawing of such a figure. Everything depends upon our acquaintance with this, and where are we to go to obtain information? There is no possible answer but one. To experience, to the originals of the present, for our knowledge of real objects; and to the different fashions in which the artists of the day reproduce these, for our knowledge of styles and of peculiarities of painting, with their special relations to the object represented.

Then comes the question, Is the artist in making his picture to alter and correct the fresco? Is he merely to find out what parts of the fresco may be said to be drawings by good artists, or is he in addition to correct at pleasure and to re-combine features or figures or groupings?

And here the employers make one last stand. 'It is absurd,' they say, 'to take the world of to-day, and to alter the picture from that. You simply invent a past which you take from the present, and you cannot tell but what the past was essentially different.'

And upon this point too the artist, if he be a wise artist, will refuse to yield. 'If I could do all that I could wish to do,' he will say, 'what you too wish should be done. But the question is not as to how much you want, but as to how much I can accomplish for you. You wish to see the real, but I know no reality save that which I see and study now for myself. You ask for truth, I know no truth but the accordance of the drawing with this my world. You wish for the removal of error, I know no error but departure from the life, as now after pains and sacrifice I see it. I am to find the causes of error? And how do I know them but by experience of the work of artists, which I compare with the reality, and so study their different styles and various deflections from the truth. It comes to this—I have no reality but one, you must have that or nothing. It may be things were different in the past; I cannot help that, I did not live then. If you object to a past brought into harmony with the present, you can have nothing from me at all.

And I do not invent a past like the present. I see many types of reality, and many styles of copying that reality. I do not say, *because* I never saw a nose or an arm like that, that *therefore* it was not so : but I do say, if any feature figure or position is neither like any I have seen, nor is a further carrying out of tendencies that I have observed, then I will never paint it so, or approve when anyone else so paints it.

And I must tell you that really there is no copying. Every man has his style, and cannot help having it. I have mine, but I have done my best to conform it to that which is true. Perhaps I have failed. You must take me or leave me.

But you must not think I am going to invent. I have the fresco as my material. From my knowledge of the real I can tell from one part often what another is, and so reconstruct the whole. From my knowledge of bad drawing I can often tell what it is has made the style vicious and the features distorted, and so can arrive at the original.

I can not do much for you. I can restore a great deal and clear away more. But again and again it will be my duty to tell you that I am powerless. Further experience may help, but after all alas ! the result may be, that of the figures of one, whom we most wish to see as he was, we can accept not one as the likeness ; and, after removal of vicious mannerisms and distortions, there is left some feeble and colourless outline of him in whose soul the ' world's broken heart,' it may be, was born again.

Note B.

The doctrine of the text supplies us with a means for judging the maxim, ' Quod ubique quod ab omnibus, etc.——verum est.'

Now is there the smallest reason to suppose that merely because the existence of a phenomenon or set of phenomena has been asserted by writers in every time, that *therefore* the phenomena are real facts ? What is the *ground* of the inference ? General consent it cannot be : if there is one belief with a greater extension than any other, it is the belief in the reality of supernatural apparitions witchcraft and sorcery. Yet the educated as a rule now reject this belief.

The question is this, Why is the fact of continual assertion a ground for belief ? It is not because the *quantity* of the witnesses precludes mistake—in these cases numbers are of little weight. It is because the coexistence of the same observation with apparently every variety of standpoint is a ground for concluding to *the quality of the basis* of the observation. The various points of view cancel each other, and the mutual obliteration of their differences affords in general some presumption that the residue, which was that which made the observation, is common to all, and therefore to us ; is in short an observation from our own point of view. This presumption of course may or may not be justified.

Whether evidence of this sort can ever be regarded as more than probable, or as valid for science, is a question which does not concern us here. For in any case the evidence would not be historical, since it would demonstrate never the particular event at a particular time ; it could never reconstruct one particular observation, but would be a general conclusion to the reality of a *class* of phenomena.

Note C.

Unless the matter of historical testimony is subject to analogy throughout all its details, the main argument of these pages is broken; and I confess that, in my opinion, that part of the discussion is the weakest. I will state the objection which occurs to me against it, and will then endeavour to show that the objection is not really valid, and to explain more fully the position taken in the text.

'What it comes to,' may be said, 'is no more than this. We have proof, and we have probability. Proof is scientific, a theoretical certainty; probability is not scientific, but it may be a practical certainty. Probability we admit must depend on analogy; but we utterly deny that the probable and the analogous are convertible terms, so that hence the non-analogous means the improbable.

*'Can analogy lead us to the non-analogous? Yes. It is only in the conjunction of the words that there is anything paradoxical. The real paradox is to identify the probable and the analogous, so as to be forced to assert that no non-analogous scientific fact can ever be probable.

'If we assure ourselves that the standpoint of an enquirer is the same as ours, we can receive as probable what he thinks probable, and without specific analogy from our own private experience. Or, taking his proved facts as certain, we ourselves may conclude by inference to a probable fact both new and non-analogous. In the field of science such results as these must be considered probable.

'And again in science, where I cannot be sure of the precise standpoint of the observer, I may yet take the facts, which are certain for him, as possessing at least probability, and these facts again not subject to analogy.

* I have throughout used 'analogy' in the ordinary sense, which prohibits our applying the term to personal observation. But, if we look closer, in the extension of our experience we use what may be considered as analogical reasoning. In observing an altogether new sort of fact, the parts of the fact are brought into the mind by subsumption under certain known heads. If it were not so we could not observe the fact at all, as it would come into no relation with our minds. This process might improperly be called 'analogy.' The fact as a whole is of course not accounted for so. It requires to be made one object by a synthetic act of the mind.

'Turning now to history, why in the world, if I partially possess myself of the witness's consciousness, may I not regard his facts, when apart from analogy, as certainly probable? To refute me you must maintain that I cannot get a probable proof by a partial identification. And this you maintain in the teeth of facts.

'And if my conclusion is probable, and if history does not go beyond probability, why is my conclusion to stand outside when others no better are admitted?

'So much for the facts, and now for the reasoning. Analogy is not to affirm the non-analogous? Nothing is easier. You start from your private experience, and you argue by analogy to a consciousness probably right in the matter of its non-analogous testimony. You get the fact of a man, whose evidence, even apart from analogy, is probably right; and then you receive as probable his testimony 'en bloc,' though supported in detail by no analogy. To the particular facts you have nothing similar, but to the main fact which contains them you have; and this main fact rests upon analogy and makes its particulars thereby probable.

'(And, briefly to illustrate, there may be supposed events in history, which, though not in contradiction with my notion of the Divinity, may yet involve attributes supported by no analogy from that idea and experience which I have. Yet on evidence I am bound to believe in these attributes, unless the others exclude them; and why cannot history prove them probably by a partial identification with the consciousness of the witness?)'

Thus far the objection. There is in it little that we can not adopt, except the particular application to history.

The problem is as follows. Let us suppose a man in the past whose point of view is equal to our own. Let us suppose that he testifies to an event in history, and further to a non-analogous event. His evidence is not scientific, because we cannot assure ourselves of the conditions of his observation. Yet his evidence amounts to a high degree of scientific probability. This case is certainly conceivable. Why then, the question arises, is that, which is probable enough for science, actually not probable enough for history?

I answer that I do not deny the mere amount of probability. I admit that the case in question may actually possess a greater probability than most of the events, than all if you will, which I make part of history; but, none the less, do I say that I will never receive that event as historical, except upon analogy from the present.

We must make a distinction. For science there is proof and there is probability; there are likely but uncertain facts, and probable but unverified hypotheses; but for science there is no such thing as a probable *conclusion*. The conclusions of science, which it takes for certainties, are never, while science is true to itself, anything short of fully proved. Science recognises theoretical but not moral probability; and it cannot do this latter, because practical probability may amount to certainty.

The conclusions of history are never proved; they are first theoretical probabilities, and secondly they are more, they are moral certainties. In history the conclusions are moral certainties; but, as history is not practical, its results must be theoretical, and hence while probable are still received as theoretical certainties.

A theoretical certainty must be taken as certain, i.e. as more than a probable conclusion. One of three things must be done then. We must either habitually consider the events in history (i.) as theoretically probable, and that means uncertain; or (ii.) as morally certain, whether with or apart from analogy; or (iii.) as morally certain only when supported by analogy.

The first course (i.) simply means that you have no history at all. For history you must have facts, you must have something you can believe in, and say of it 'this was so.' The mind must feel itself at home in the past; and it cannot do that when the past is represented by nothing but a present of doubtfully-weighed probabilities. History here is a word without meaning; yet history there ever must be; and let it be a delusion or not, we at least assume that it is not so.

If history exists it must be more than uncertain. We pass to the second question (ii.), and ask is history to be considered as (morally) theoretically certain, and that independent of analogy? The historical order is here an hypothesis or theory which is taken as true. Let us reflect on the result of receiving as true a conclusion in history apart from present scientific analogy.

This conclusion is not scientific, for it is not proved but only probable. For science the facts and the conclusions from the facts are not admitted as realities; and yet for history these same facts are certain. This means that what is true, what you believe, what is a fact, what really has happened, at the same time is not true, may not be believed, is not yet a fact, and cannot be said to have happened. The collision is inevitable, since the facts are the property of both spheres alike. The theorist of course may keep up the distinctions, and may never forget the saving clauses; but for the practical historian or man of science this is simply impossible. The whole interest of history is to have one truth one reality, then as now, and now as then. One course or another must be taken. Either against the scientific conscience, and to the loss of science, the historical reality must become the scientific reality; and that means that the un-analogous hypotheses and traditional facts must be received into science as verified certainties, with their consequences developed in every direction, to provoke a collision at each new discovery—or else (and this must be the better alternative) scientific evidence is made the criterion, and historical testimony subjected throughout and in all its details to analogy from that. This is the real interest of history, to find what it knows under other aspects. This is the method, and this alone, by which to avoid the struggle of truth against truth and reality against reality—a collision intolerable to the oneness of the mind which bears the distraction. The third way (iii.) is thus the only course possible to save us from scepticism in history or from credulity in science. It is the one path open to the practical critic; and this is the justification of a suspension of judgment in presence of even more than a sufficient probability. Suspension of judgment is however exclusion from history.

Long as this note has become there are yet two points which deserve our attention. The first is merely an illustration from legal proceedings. Let us suppose in a criminal case that, to prove the theory of the prisoner's guilt, an attested fact must be taken as true, though the judge and the jury are aware of nothing analogous. Speaking as one who is ignorant of law, I venture to think that on no common evidence would the prisoner be convicted. Scientific witnesses would be required; and, if their testimony was insufficient for an actual enlargement of the experience of the jury and the judge, I do not see how a conclusion could be come to. Yet, while legal is stronger as a rule than historical evidence, still legal are weaker in one way than historical conclusions. A verdict is an opinion of particular persons on a particular case; a fact in history is a past reality. This difference comes from the difference of the interest.

The second point is what seems an inconsistency in historical practice. The probability, which actually itself would not be taken into history, nevertheless is used as the basis of an analogy for theorizing tradition into an historical fact. For instance the probable evidence of past stigmatization (which would not, in default of present analogy, prove the historical fact) would perhaps and by some persons, if it were present, be made to justify the affirmation in history of the existence of stigmata. I must doubt whether this course is critical; but it is important as showing the interest of history, which moulds the past after the present, and for which the present probability is at once a canon, simply because it is present.

Note D.

It would be a serious mistake to suppose, because at a certain time criticism is not justified in considering an event historical, that *therefore* criticism will *never* be able to affirm it. There are several instances to the contrary.

Herodotus records the account of the circumnavigation of Africa (iv. 42), and does not believe it, because it contained a fact which to him seemed incredible, since utterly without analogy (as he thought) in the astronomical world (Ελεγον εμοι μεν ου πιστα αλλῳ δε δη τεῳ, ὡς περιπλωοντες την Λιβυην ἥλιον εσχον ες τα δεξια). This very circumstance, as the commentators remark on the passage, is the best evidence for the truth of the Phœnicians' story.

The accounts of stigmatization furnish another example. It was clearly impossible for the critical historian to receive this testimony in the absence of any present scientific analogy. But if (as seems likely) such analogy exists; if the possibility of the phenomenon can be scientifically proved, the case as to the medieval stories is at once altered; and their possible reception becomes a mere question of the amount and quality of the historical evidence.

Again, in the face of admitted strong historical evidence, Gibbon (cap. xxxvii.) declined to believe that the African confessors spoke without tongues. Gibbon was unquestionably right; since he had before him nothing analogous. It turns out now to be the fact however, and is said to be proved by repeated scientific experiments, that speech is possible after the total excision of the tongue. The attitude of the historian to the supposed miracle must now of course be different, and the testimony may be received and weighed.

The rule for the critical historian is always to keep on the side of safety. It is better to suspend the judgment and be wrong, than to be right against reason and in the face of science.

Note E.

Everything, we have said, depends on personal experience. And this means that when pressed we must come to, and must start from that; must from the ground of that connect our self with past selves, so as to know what once on a time was fact for them; and so as to know that it also is fact for us now, because in respect of the class of phenomena in question, their consciousness is identical with ours. In critical history we either perform this operation ourselves, or we take it for granted that it has been or could be done.

And with the phrases of 'personal observation and experience' we have said enough doubtless, if that were our object, to satisfy most persons, or at least to stop their mouths. But a man who enquires will wish to go farther.

'I know well,' he may say, 'that fresh observation and facts are supposed to give the basis from which to correct or make valid the old material. But what I do not see is how on your standpoint such a position is possible.

'You say that all is inferential. This must mean that, as are the the premises of the inference, so also are the conclusions. To get beyond your premises is surely impossible; and as for correcting them, that is nonsense.

'Come to the facts. It is notorious that a man may be quite incapable of receiving essentially and vitally new facts in their essential and vital meaning. He *will* subsume them under his own categories; he .must make them members of his world, or not take them in at all. As is the man, so are his facts. Uneducated persons and children transform to their own likeness all they assimilate: and savages are in many cases literally unable to take in what to us seem simple impressions of passivity, for this sufficient reason that they have no internal world which answers to them, no premises under which to subsume them.

'What it comes to is this. A man has a certain world to start with, and he doesn't know how he has got it: this world contains every sort of matter historical and otherwise. '*Personal observation!*' What on earth does '*personal*' mean, when the contents of his person, his personal world, is already traditional and decidedly not his in particular? And what sense is there in sending him to 'observation,' when that only enlarges but cannot correct or innovate, for the simple reason that what is not in harmony excludes itself from observation? This 'personal experience' is a mere superstition, for nothing is more personal to any man than the traditional world already personal within him.

'You have used 'inference' to knock down 'fact'; and now from 'fact' you want to start to get a basis for inference. But all facts are alike in being inferential, and therefore alike in this, that they issue from and are based on the given.'

The objection is well worth considering in itself, and comes to this, 'How is critical observation and experience possible?' This is a somewhat wide question, and we make not the smallest profession of discussing it here. And we are not obliged to discuss it. It may seem that we are so: it may seem that we have rested on critical experience, and are therefore bound to explain its possibility.

This is quite wrong. What we wanted to show was this, that *given* the existence of history, it must be critical; and that *if* it is critical, that *then* it must rest on present critical experience. That is our whole conclusion, and if any one chooses to argue, 'There is no *critical* experience, and therefore no *critical* history,' we shall not contend with him, but merely add 'and therefore no history at all,' and treat his subsequent historical dogmatism with silent contempt.

Not for the sake of our argument then do we feel bound to consider the objection we have developed; but entirely for the sake of the subject of the objection itself are we willing to say something; not much, but not much less than what we have learnt.

In the sharpest form of the difficulty it comes to the old crux, 'knowledge implies previous knowledge,' or 'subsumption previous subsumption,' and is directed against the possibility of any beginning, and hence against the existence of knowledge at all.

It is impossible to attempt to deal with this here. Nor does it touch the particular case. We are not treating of the beginning of knowledge and experience in general, but find ourselves on a problem in the middle of the stream.

As it touches us the problem is this; 'Since you start from the given, and rest on the given, which at all events *may* come to you as uncriticized and uncritical—*how* are you to criticize it? How *from* what is given get to that which is critical, when the source and instrument vitiates the outcome, when the unsurveyed foundation damns the edifice? If you tell a superstitious man to observe *personally*, do you really think that he will observe critically? Only the critical mind is capable of critical observation, and a mind full of uncritical matter can not possibly be critical.'

It is a hard question, but we must try to answer. We must bear in mind that in the growth of knowledge there are two sides. On one side we have the given whole, the world, or the consciousness, or the self—briefly that which is *so far* the real. And now under this we bring fresh facts. We subsume them under that which we have, and we are; and this means that they become a part of the whole, which *therefore*, and as over against the *former* world, is a fresh whole.

But we shall be cut short here. 'This is not to the purpose. What you want is to get a split between fresh observation and the old world, and you can't do it this way. You forget that the facts not already of a piece with the system are *not* subsumed, and hence the whole may be overlooked but is never criticized. It only grows like the lower forms of nature by accretion and not by evolution, by simple addition of new material and not by a process of differentiation and integration.'

We resume. And it doubtless is true that in some individuals, and in some countries and times, to a certain extent this is the case. If it always were true, then there would be no criticism nor any critical observation. But as a matter of fact humanity does not grow in this way and it cannot. And what is the reason of this? Where is it that the description of progress as growth by accretion is incorrect? When is a split between new and old a possibility?

When the old involves a contradiction; i.e. when, supposing itself to be a system, it in reality is not consistent. Then that which is subsumed under it will also be inconsistent, inconsistent with the old and also with itself. The contradictory elements will be exhibited in their freedom, and, by the particularization of fresh subsumption, and by growing divergencies in consciousness, will contradict the unity of consciousness. The uneasiness will cause reflection on the object or stage of consciousness (both are the same), and then an alienation and rejection.

'But in this what about the new personal observation? Are not the system and its particular subsumptions all negated alike?' They are; and it is possible that, turning away from both old and new, the mind may suspend itself dissatisfied, and here again the critical experience be wanting.

But the mind is such an unity that it holds a contradiction in itself until the divided elements cohere, are solved and blended into another consciousness, a fresh system, a new world; new and which contains the old in a transformed shape.

And this is why (to begin with 'personal') that the personality is wanted; for that is no less than the principle of synthesis which makes this new world.

'Let all this be true,' it will still be rejoined, 'you have got a split between the reflecting person and the old world. But what of experience and observation? What have they to do with your new synthesis, your new object, your re-systematized world?'

Patience! I reply. The new synthesis is not yet a world, but an embryo world; and further the new principle, which has resulted from the negation of the old, may either be itself an object *for* consciousness, or may be merely a consciousness which is not yet aware of itself; i.e. it may be a new doctrine, that we are aware of, and go forth to realize against the old, or may be the changed attitude of mind that knows itself as yet only as the denial of the old world, and must have a new world to know what itself is.

In the former case it is a conscious principle, but abstract and undeveloped; and it is a new object, but still subjective, not yet evolved nor known in its determinations. You want to know what this new world is in the concrete? You must see for yourself. Subsume particulars under it; fill it with matter, and you will see. Realize it, and you will find what it is you have realized. That is why personal observation is wanted.

The old matter of the old system is vitiated throughout, because vitalized by a defunct theory. You want sound matter, and you get it by subsuming under principles which you feel to be true. Thus you make a system the principle and details of which are both known to you. And now you can re-systematize the material of the old world. You could not do it before because the old world was so particularized that nothing abstract could reorganize its details. You wanted a principle truly particularized into the concrete, and, now you have that, you can proceed, remembering that the new object is the real object, and the old powerless before it.

Or, in the second case, the new consciousness is not aware of itself. It knows itself only as the self, for which the old world is inadequate and alien; it feels the impulse to find itself anew in another world; but it has no principle under which it consciously subsumes; the self which subsumes is not, as self, an object of consciousness. It *finds* a fresh object, it *sees* a new world grow up before it, and it thinks of itself as the passive and reflecting mirror. By observation it gets its new world, and from that it learns the nature of itself. It gets the consciousness of the principle which was the unknown agent at work, and then from that basis it can proceed to re-include the old rejected elements.

So far we have considered that progress which involves a breach with the existing world. But we have yet the case before us where it is the finding of new facts which seems to overthrow a hitherto unsuspected creed, and premises sound in themselves.

We must go back for a space. We first saw how the mind, as a world or system, finds itself in an object of like nature : we saw how it was a contradiction involved in the consciousness which made the subsumed object contradictory; and next how the mind, as unity, rose above its own contradiction, and reflected on and negated its former stage of consciousness or world.

But such conscious reflection is by no means the normal process of empirical developement; and, as often as not, the old is not negated till it is found existing peacefully side by side with a new state of things, which has got there Heaven knows how. How did it got there ?

It is the unconscious reflective action and systematization of the mind which has made it. The proceeds of experience are contradictory, and the mind is a principle of unity. It feels the contradictions, and, without knowing it, is more or less alienated from its contents, but comes to no downright breach with the world. On the contrary it imagines itself to be bringing all new details faithfully under the old world or old self; and it does not know that *itself* is the active principle of subsumption, and that it no longer is one with the former self. From that old self it separates itself more and more, developes and partially solves its contradictions, critically corrects its one-sidednesses, rules out its inconsistencies with unconscious but incessant activity; and all the time is subsuming new matter under this innovating and perpetually growing self.* The assimilated details, it is obvious, no longer will bear the character, and form the counterpart of the old self, but show more and more in their developement the results of the mind's unconscious work; and, being subsumed into the new self, react powerfully upon it to increased separation from the former stage of consciousness, and to

* We may consider the process as taking place in one and the same mind, or series of minds; but in reality the differentiation of the old system of belief is accelerated by the diversity of individualities. In an inconsistent substance the inconsistencies are explicated by being more or less fixed, in different individuals, as one-sided personalities. The collision of these is an instigation to the general mind to recover and re-collect itself from them into a consistent centre of integration.

the production of fresh facts which are still less in harmony with the old system of belief.

All this time however the subsuming self, as in a succession of fresh individuals it gets farther and farther removed, still thinks itself loyal to the ancient creed, which really is rapidly becoming (or may even in parts or altogether have become) a traditional mass, a semi-effete stage of consciousness, an organism from which the life has been drawn by a younger organism to feed itself, a dead or half-dead self existing in and alongside of a new world and a new self. At this epoch the smallest shock, any extra-contradiction between the two lives, a sudden discovery, or in short any accident will force upon the mind the consideration of what it really is, and the startling and appalling revelation that it has two selves and a double world. Whether a contest ensues will depend on how far the soul has been withdrawn from the elder organism, and how far the younger has appropriated to itself all sides of the reality. But in any case the victory will lie with the new (though the new may be forced in the struggle to extend and modify itself); since it is the self which pleads and judges its own cause, and, after vehement reaction (it may be), and violent rejection of the old, the traditional mass, the effete organism will itself be assimilated, and live once more in the new and re-integrated body.

If the further question be put, 'What necessity is there for the given world to be self-contradictory? this note must certainly be kept within bounds; but briefly an answer might be given, which appears the best to give. The universe seems to be one system; it is an organism (it would appear) and more. It bears the character of the self, the personality to which it is relative, and without which for us it is as good as nothing. Hence any portion of the universe by itself can not be a consistent system; for it refers to the whole, and has the whole present in it. Potentially the whole (since embodying that which is actually the whole), in trying to fix itself as itself, it succeeds only in laying stress on its character of relativity; it is carried beyond and contradicts itself. Or more briefly thus. Evolution is necessary because the mind is actually limited, virtually unlimited; and the object lives in the life of the mind and varies with it.

To sum the result. 'Go to *experience*' does not *here* imply respect for one class of facts alone. You go to experience to know what facts in general are, since the only way to realize your principle, to know what your premises are, what your system is and is to be, is to subsume matter under it. And 'Go to *personal* experience' is essential, not because, as this or that man, you are better than anybody else who is or has been; but, just as experience is necessary to get facts for your principle, and tell you what it is, so *you* must form the matter by subsumption in order to know that it has been subsumed under *your* principle, and is therefore *a fact for you.*

No facts but my facts; and only through my facts do I realize myself, and know what I am. Personal observation does not mean that this or that sensuous matter comes into relation with this or that sensuous individual. To imagine that in this is to be found the smallest guarantee or test of truth, is a wretched superstition, a proof of the most utter philosophical uneducatedness, and that completest blindness to the experience of everyday life which is possible only to a vicious a priori dogmatism. 'Experience' means the verification in the concrete, and the bringing to consciousness (formally or in detail) of our known or unknown actuating principle and presupposition; and 'personal' means that our world is to be an unity answering to our oneness—it means the emphasis of the idea of system in a new man.

T. HAILING, PRINTER, CHELTENHAM.

MR. SIDGWICK'S HEDONISM:

AN EXAMINATION OF

THE MAIN ARGUMENT OF

"THE METHODS OF ETHICS"

BY

F. H. BRADLEY

FELLOW OF MERTON COLLEGE, OXFORD

HENRY S. KING AND CO., LONDON

1877

OXFORD:

BY E. PICKARD HALL AND J. H. STACY,

PRINTERS TO THE UNIVERSITY.

PREFACE.

THE following pages are intended to supply, not a general review or estimate of the 'Methods of Ethics,' but an examination of the main argument of that work, the thesis it supports, and the steps by which it goes to its conclusion.

The position which Mr. Sidgwick's book has taken in the literature of the day fully justifies the length of this examination. The remarks which I found space to make in my Ethical Studies were, I fear, too brief and condensed to express my objections. And I think that a discussion of the subject in detail can hardly fail to be of use to the student of Moral Philosophy.

From the first I have found Mr. Sidgwick's book not easy to understand, and it is probable that in some points I may have misapprehended his meaning. My own belief is that Mr. Sidgwick's argument is in itself not clear, and that the obscurity arises from the omission on his part of any serious attempt to arrive at an understanding of the fundamental preconceptions with which he operates. In this the reader may find I am mistaken; but I cannot doubt that the enquiry, if it does not prove the edifice unstable, will at least bring more clearly into light the nature of the foundation. And this will be a result well worth the labour.

What I have tried to do is, first of all, at the price, I fear, of a great deal of tediousness, to help the reader to master the most prominent conceptions of the book, and to bring to light the obscurity and ambiguous nature of the leading terms; and the equivocal character of the main thesis. Then in Part II. I have entered on the proof of the thesis which is offered, and have endeavoured to show that it is unsatisfactory. Lastly, in Part III. § 8, I have tried to exhibit the real nature of the author's proposed Ethical Science, and to point out some of the objections to which it lies open: and in § 9 I have discussed the problem, partly moral and partly theological, which is raised at the end of Mr. Sidgwick's work. Some general remarks on the 'objective' character of morality have been excluded from want of space.

TABLE OF CONTENTS.

Part I.—The Definitions.

§ I.—*Reason.*

No one, I think, who reads the Methods of Ethics can fail to be struck by the recurrence of the word 'reasonable.' Plainly it is a term we ought to understand, for the Right, the Good, the End, the Desirable, all seem to fall under it[1] and to depend on it for their meaning. It is scarcely saying too much when we say that Mr. Sidgwick's main thesis stands and falls with his view of the 'reasonable.' But when we ask, Has the word been explained with sufficient clearness? I think the answer must be, No.

What is reason? It is defined (27) as 'a faculty which takes cognizance of objective truth.' We shall have to ask hereafter what 'objective' in general means, but here 'objective truth' seems opposed to 'purely subjective phenomena,' 'the sensations of the sentient being' (23), and is 'the same, whether recognised or not, for all Minds or Subjects' (182)[2].

---

[1] There can be no doubt that 'reasonable,' 'right,' 'ought' all stand for the same idea (29), and as little doubt that 'preferable,' 'desirable,' 'the end' are equivalent. True, 'good' can be distinguished from 'right,' but for our purpose the distinction seems to be of no importance, and (as applied to conduct) they 'coincide substantially' (98). Indeed (80, note) we hear of '"right" and "reasonable," and the equivalent phrase "what ought to be" [done or aimed at]'. I am not sure whether 'good' and 'reasonable' are ever coupled, but the end is the 'end of reason,' and the good is the rational end or ends. It would tend to clearness if we were told at the beginning which of these terms are convertible, or at all events whether we have to do with one or more than one 'fundamental notion.'

[2] It is right that I should say here that I cannot reconcile with this Mr. Sidgwick's view as to Egoism being reasonable. See below, p. 36, note, and p. 51.

But in what way does reason apprehend truth ? Is it merely 'discursive?' No, 'it seems . . . to belong to reason not merely to judge of the relation of means to ends, or of the consistency of maxims : but also to determine the ultimate ends and true first principles of action' (26). This 'operation' is 'intuitive.'

Reason, so far, is not merely discursive but also 'intuitive ;' and the question which remains is as to the nature of the 'objective truth' which it apprehends. For

'we do not say, in physics, that individual facts are apprehended by the Reason : we consider this faculty to be conversant in its discursive operation with the relation of judgments or propositions; and the intuitive reason (which is here rather in question) we restrict to the apprehension of universal truths, such as the axioms of logic and mathematics. Now, as I shall presently notice, it is not uncommonly held that the moral faculty judges primarily of individual cases, applying directly to these the general notion of Duty, and deciding intuitively what ought to be done by this person in these particular circumstances. On this view the moral apprehension is more analogous to Sense-Perception than to Rational Intuition (as commonly understood) : and hence the term Moral Sense has been preferred by many, who did not mean to suggest thereby any scepticism as to the reality of moral (as distinct from psychological) truth. But it is so important to avoid this suggestion, that it seems better to use generally the term Reason : provided it be not supposed to mean anything more specific than "a faculty which takes cognizance of objective truth."' (26-7.)

We find, however, that it does hereafter mean something more specific. We find (85) that, in speaking of 'the popular view of Conscience,' our writer says :—

'This view may be called ultra-intuitional, as it recognizes simple immediate intuitions alone and rejects all modes of reasoning to moral conclusions. But it may equally well be called ultra-empirical as it emphasizes the authority of particular moral experiences in comparison with universal rules or axioms. This then we may describe as one phase or variety of the Intuitional method, involving really a negation of method, and excluding what is more strictly called Reason from moral decisions.'

And then comes this note to the word Reason, 'i.e. the faculty of apprehending universal truth.'

It would appear then that in future we have to deal with a strict and a loose use of Reason, but I cannot find that in the sequel, when Reason comes in, we are clearly told *which* Reason is meant. On this point I have found Mr. Sidgwick very hard to understand, but I will try to put before the reader what seems to be his doctrine.

I think that Reason stands for the faculty which apprehends 'universal truth,' 'general rules,' 'abstract moral notions,' 'moral axioms' (87): and further that it includes as well the *reasoning* to particular cases from 'general moral maxims' whether these latter are 'universal moral intuitions' (190) or not. The word *may* cover more, but I doubt it.

Now (this is an important matter) is 'conscience,' in the sense of a judgment on particular cases (85), irrational? I think not. 'Even when the decision of the moral faculty is felt to relate primarily to some particular action, we cannot really exclude generality from the notion of the action thus judged to be right' (86). 'The moral truth apprehended will be intrinsically universal, though particular in our first apprehension of it' (*ibid.*). And (189) we find that all moral judgments have a 'potential universality.' The result seems to be that 'conscience' is not irrational; but it certainly is 'unreasoned.' 'Reflective conscientious persons' are 'inclined to bring' each case under some general rule (*ibid.*).

In both cases, of the immediate and the reflective conscience alike, I take it that reason gives, or at least apprehends, the general; but the latter case is 'reasoned;' there is an explicit reasoning which brings the particular as an instance. under the universal rule. Then what are we to say about the former case? In what sense is reason present in non-reflective conscience? Does reason here give a product in which both elements exist but are not distinguished? Is reason here in a 'potential' or 'intrinsical' or 'latent' state in which it gives an individual intuition? That is one view. Or are we to say that this intuition in which the two elements are not made explicit is not really reason at all? That is another view. On this 'potentially universal' would mean that you can by reflection separate the two elements implicit in the individual judgment, and then the universal element, when explicit, is apprehended by reason, though not before[1]. But which view is our author's I cannot say.

I am afraid that this discussion may appear to the reader mere verbal trifling, but he will find, I think, on reflection, that the subject of 'potential universality' calls for a clearer explanation than it has received, and again that it is a most important matter to know whether reason apprehends the individual or only the general. When we come to argue from the nature of reason to the nature of the end, this difference must seriously affect our conclusion. But for the present all we can say is that what is true for reason seems in the main to be that which is true in general or in the abstract.

§ 2.—*Practical Reason.*

So far we have had to do with reason as cognitive, and, now we are come to practical reason, the light grows dimmer and dimmer, and we see little more than that we are encountered by at least some of the difficulties of Kant's ethical dualism.

'The real end of Reason' is the same as 'the absolutely good' (391); but how can *reason* give an *end?* 'The Moral Reason is a Spring of Action' (x). Reason 'dictates.' 'Reason prompts us to a certain kind of action' (29–30). Reason has '"a categorically imperative" function' (24). So far there seems to be no doubt.

'Acting rationally' is acting 'from an impulse in harmony with an intellectual apprehension of an objective rule, or intrinsically desirable end' (43). 'That in us which claims

---

[1] I fail to understand Mr. Sidgwick when (27) he speaks of a view which holds that 'the moral faculty judges primarily of individual cases, applying directly to these the general notion of Duty, and deciding intuitively what ought to be done by this person in these particular circumstances.' His language here implies that the general notion is explicit, and that to some extent the judgment is reflective; but this can hardly be what he means to say.

authority is never a mere sentiment, but always a faculty
cognisant of an objective rule or imperative which exists
independently of its effect on our feelings, and such a faculty
is what we must mean by Reason' (62). 'There actually is
found in man a certain impulse to do what is reasonable as
such' (x). There is a 'central desire to do Right as such'
(347).

But what does all this mean? I confess I cannot say.
Reason seems to be 'a spring of action' in this sense, that
when reason says, Something ought to be done, then there
goes with that a desire to do what reason orders. So much
seems clear, but it does not tell us how reason can order.

Are we to say that in practical reason thought and will
are united in such a way that the object of this faculty is no
mere *fact* which we recognize, but an *end*, an idea which in us
calls for its reality? Then what need for an adventitious desire
to turn reason into a 'spring of action'? Are we to say that
practical reason is *made* practical by this desire, that the addition of this desire to theoretic reason constitutes practical
reason? This does not seem to be our author's view. For

'It is enough if it be granted that there exists in all moral
agents as such a permanent desire ... to do what is right or reasonable because it is such: so that when our practical reason recognizes
any course of conduct as right, this desire immediately impels us
with a certain force towards such conduct.' (27.)

Clearly then, even apart from the desire, reason is still
practical, though not perhaps 'a spring of action.'

But then how can reason give an *end?* How can it
'prompt' or 'dictate' or be 'categorically imperative'? Is
there, beside the desire which makes it a 'spring,' *another*
desire which makes it practical? If so, what is it after all
which gives the end? If not so, how can reason 'prescribe'
and order, as well as perceive? Is to be 'cognisant of an
imperative' the same thing as to give an order?

It is possible that our author's view may be that desire
gives the end, while reason qualifies it. *What* the end is
reason does not know, but, *given* the end, it further deter-
mines its nature, and so brings into play a third element, the

'central desire to do Right as such.' If so, the end is hardly the 'end of Reason,' and reason is no more categorical, but hypothetical, or at best, with co-ordinate authority. But I do not think this is what Mr. Sidgwick means.

The following questions I think need an answer. Is reason nothing but 'the slave of the passions'? Does desire give the end and reason calculate the means? Certainly our author does not hold this. Does reason desire or will? This again he seems reluctant to affirm. But if it does not desire and will, how can the end be the end of reason? If reason is no more than 'cognisant of an imperative,' how is it practical? Is my reason practical when I read an Act of Parliament? Does my sight 'prompt' or 'dictate' when I see a police notice on the wall? When I hear the word Forward, are my ears 'categorically imperative'?

Does reason tell you what to do, or does it tell you only what you are told to do? Does it give orders, or do no more than carry them? And then *whose* orders does it carry?

To explain our *obedience* to the order by bringing in a desire for the reasonable does not help us at all. The question is not, Does an emotion attend the *recognition* of a mere fact. For in morality we have not to do with a mere fact, with this or that command which is prescribed from without, seen perhaps by reason, and then obeyed by desire and will: nor, I think, does our author hold this. In morality we prescribe to and dictate to ourselves. We do not perceive that there *is* an order, we *give* that order, and we *put* an end before ourselves to be done. And how can reason do this? If we abstract from desire and will, what is left of 'end' and 'ought' and 'imperative'? Has 'This is my *end*' any sense when desire is kept out, or comes in but to say '*And* I will do it'? Does not end mean will, and my end my will?

I can find no answers to these questions in the Methods of Ethics. It is not fair to our author, I admit, to ask him for a psychology which he does not undertake to give. It is fair to point out that the psychological doctrine, which (whatever it may be) he most undeniably does put forward, is either wholly obscure, or else labours under well-known difficulties which are not met, but which, if not met, must gravely affect his thesis.

The question of this section, if we put it from the other end, is, What is the relation of desire to the desirable? and that word leads us to the following section.

§ 3.—*The Desirable and Pleasure.*

I am afraid the reader will be tired already by these questions about words, but we can not go on until we have asked what 'desirable' means. In ordinary English it is the same as what 'is to be' or 'should be desired,' but it *may* also stand for that which simply can be desired, or does excite desire. The latter usage, I believe, has no place in our spoken language, and even in literature perhaps is obsolete, but still it exists. How does Mr. Sidgwick use the word?

When it appears in his writing apart from its connection with ethical questions I think it *always* bears the first sense. But what is its more technical meaning? Passages (at the foot of pp. 137, 318) show that it is not equivalent to 'desired'; and (93 note) we find ' " Good "=" intrinsically preferable or desirable," ' and again (391) we hear of 'the real end of Reason, the absolutely Good or Desirable.' Clearly then desirable or preferable=good or end (cf. 60, 133, 183).

Nor can the phrases 'intrinsically,' 'absolutely,' 'objectively,' 'ultimately,' 'in itself' be taken to differentiate desirable and good, for they are applied to both; 'the ultimate end, or entity, regarded as intrinsically good and desirable' (66; cf. 369, 391, 392 note). And moreover we find 'good' and 'desirable' coupled without qualification (95 last line; cf. 94, 369), and (9) 'desirable' is used as one notion with 'intrinsically good,' or 'end which Reason regards as ultimate.'

So far we see that 'desirable'='good' or 'end.'

'Let then pleasure be defined as feeling that is preferable or desirable, considered merely as feeling' (118). 'Pleasure being defined as "feeling judged to be preferable or desirable considered merely as feeling"' (xii). 'To mean by Pleasure only Preferable or Desirable Feeling of whatever kind' (372). 'Happiness, or the sum of such feelings as, at the time that they are felt, are immediately known to be intrinsically desirable' (368). Mark here '*intrinsically*.' 'The kind of feeling which is most pleasant or preferable as feeling' (162).

What is all this? The end of the argument being to show that pleasure and good are the same, is it possible that here at the beginning we have 'good' and 'end' inserted into the definition of pleasure? I think we shall find this really is the case. The audacious *petitio principii* which commended itself to Mr. Mill (365), is perhaps more veiled in our author's pages, but through its thin disguise we recognize the old cause of our errors, the unconscious equivocation by which desirable means indifferently, What I like, or, What I ought to like, just as the conclusion suggests[1].

I think the reader will search in vain for any passage in which Mr. Sidgwick discriminates these two meanings of 'desirable.' In his argument it is the second which is prominent, but in his definition of pleasure he has the first in view; if, that is to say, he really does in his own mind distinguish between them. Let us see what the definition of pleasure is.

Pleasure is 'the kind of feeling which pleases us, which we like or prefer[2]' (114). In short, it is 'agreeable sensation' (33, 41) or 'agreeable feeling' (x).

So far we have seen that desirable or preferable can pass either for pleasant or good, and so is a ready means for iden-

---

[1] It is interesting to see that in his remarks on Mr. Mill's proof of Utilitarianism, our author calls attention to the fact that in this 'desirable'=what one *ought* to desire (365), and instructive to notice that he seems unaware of Mr. Mill's equivocation. He understands the latter writer to make an *inference* 'from the universal desiredness to the desirability of Happiness' (366); against which interpretation I will simply refer the reader to the passage as Mr. Sidgwick himself quotes it (365).

[2] I am anxious not to disturb the exposition by avoidable criticism, but I must point out that to insert the conception of *preference* into the definition of pleasure seems wholly indefensible.

tifying these terms. And now we must ask more narrowly as to this pleasure which is the end for Hedonism.

Pleasure we saw was feeling that is desirable as feeling, and now what is feeling? That question must be answered before we can proceed.

We hear (76–7) of a 'certain state or quality of the consciousness of the agent which we call Pleasure or Satisfaction,' and this leads us to doubt, first, whether pleasure be a feeling or the quality of a feeling[1], and second, whether feeling is the same as consciousness. The latter point is of great importance because, as we know, there is no psychical phenomenon whatever which 'consciousness' has not been used to cover.

Pleasure (389) is 'to include the highest and most refined kinds of preferable or desirable consciousness.' Happiness is 'the most pleasant consciousness conceivable' (19). 'Happiness was explained to be preferable or desirable feeling or consciousness' (369). And (78) we see 'a pleasure' may mean 'a whole state of consciousness which is only partly pleasurable.'

Of course if our author likes to identify consciousness and feeling he has a right to do so, but then we have a right to ask him to be consistent in his usage. This I think he is not.

We find (52; cf. 164) that 'passive' and 'active consciousness' are distinguished, and the former identified with 'pleasure or pain or desire or aversion.' 'Changes in the train of ideas and feelings that constitutes our conscious life' (52). 'Conscious existence, the stream of action and feeling' (102). 'Conscious life includes besides actions the whole range of feeling' (103). And. (179) action and feeling are distinguished. Again (131–2) 'cognitive' consciousness is distinguished from 'presentative consciousness,' and further the latter from feeling[2].

[1] See below, p. 16, and 30, note.

[2] I am not sure whether it has any bearing on the subject, but in fairness I should say that (164) Mr. Sidgwick distinguishes 'our faculties' from 'the mental phenomena which result from their exercise,' of which latter alone we are 'directly cognisant' (cf. 193). The faculties I take to be the same as the

In short, while on the one hand feeling and consciousness seem convertible, on the other hand consciousness is by far the wider term, and covers the whole self. We find (171) 'life or consciousness;' and the result of this somewhat loose terminology is that instead of 'agreeable sensation or feeling' we can write if we please 'desirable conscious life.' And this is no mere inference of our own, but, as we shall see, Mr. Sidgwick does actually do it in the very crisis of his argument (373). Must we not say then that as in 'desirable' we had a *petitio principii,* so now in the wavering phrase 'consciousness,' which is the same as feeling, and yet includes thought and action, and which enables us to write Life for the sake of life, instead of Pleasure for pleasure's sake, we have a considerable *ignoratio elenchi ?*

I think we must say this, but we must add that the confusion slides in in the argument, and that in the definition our author avoids it. Returning now to the subject of pleasure let us ask in what sense is this defined to be the end ?

The vital point is this. Is *the pleasant* the end? or, Is *pleasure* the end? The former question we may answer in the affirmative and yet be not one step nearer Hedonism. But if we say, The end is pleasure as distinct from that which is pleasant, then that is Hedonism. And our author does answer the question so. He does not say clearly whether mere pleasure is a feeling or only the quality of a feeling, though the latter seems to be his doctrine (76-7); but this distinction is I think of little importance here. Mr. Sidgwick is perfectly clear on these points that 'Feeling cannot be conceived to exist otherwise than as it is felt—its manner of existence is its being felt' (117). 'The pleasantness of

'possibilities' or 'tendencies' (whatever they are) which, in addition to the 'actual existence,' i. e. 'particular states,' constitute our being (102-3). I give this view because I feel so little at home with Mr. Sidgwick that I cannot say whether it may not be relevant here. But in any case the confusion would remain. For while as we saw on the one hand feeling = consciousness; we have again 'the transitory phenomena' (which appear to be the 'effects' of the 'possibilities') described as 'actions or feelings' (193). So again 'feeling or cognition' (23; cf. 102-3, 170).

the feeling is a purely subjective fact' (116). We are to 'separate in thought any state of consciousness from all its objective circumstances and conditions . . . and contemplate it merely as the transient feeling of a single subject' (*ibid.*). 'All pleasures are understood to be so called because they have a common property of pleasantness, and may therefore be compared in respect of this common property' (78). The end is 'the sum of pleasures valued in proportion to their pleasantness' (xi). And from p. 116 we see that pleasantness is the one preferable quality of any state of consciousness when considered as mere feeling.

The end is the pleasantness of pleasant feelings, and the greatest surplus of that to the whole creation, 'the innumerable multitude of living beings, present and to come' (373). The end is not the pleasant merely; that which is pleasant is only a means to the end, and, strictly speaking, nothing is the end but pleasantness and the maximum surplus of that.

This is the thesis which our author has to maintain, and before I go on to criticise it I should like to point out that we have already got the means of proving something very like it. If we write '*an* end' for '*the* end,' and leave out 'maximum surplus,' we can demonstrate thus.

Happiness or pleasure is desirable feeling or consciousness, and what is desirable is good or end, therefore pleasure is end or good. And the desirable or good must be reasonable, which means universal or at least objective, hence pleasure is an end as universal or objective, i.e. not as the pleasure of this or that man but as pleasure in general. So far we demonstrate from our definitions. And to prove our whole thesis we may add, Is there anything desirable but conscious life, or even life? But pleasure is that, and that is pleasure. So pleasure is *the* one end. Further, since you cannot distinguish pleasures by quality, you must do it by quantity, and hence maximum of pleasure is the end. Q. E. D.

And the moral of this section is that a good definition saves argument.

§ 4.—*The End.*

The end is 'the sum of pleasures valued in proportion to their pleasantness,' and we have now to criticise this. For further remarks on the subject I must refer to my Ethical Studies, but there are two main points which I cannot pass over; one the possibility of comparing the pleasantness of pleasures, and the other the nature of the greatest sum.

I. And first it would appear that the abstraction of pleasantness from the pleasant, in order to the pursuit of a maximum of the former, is impossible to execute. You cannot abstract and compare so as to arrange the world of pleasant things in an order of quantitative pleasantness.

The question, I take it, is *not* whether by abstraction you can have a science of quantity in general, nor again whether in particular you are *ever* able to say one feeling is more pleasant than another. There is no dispute between me and Mr. Sidgwick on either of these points. The facts are obvious. The question *is*, (1) whether you can compare *all* pleasures in this way, and (2) whether you can compare *any* pleasures, so as to express them as quantities of units of pleasantness, reduced to the same denomination. Can you add and substract pleasures, and say, This lot will be greater, and so much greater, than that lot?

If you cannot do this latter, if you can only, taking any two pleasures, say, One is greater than the other, but can give neither the quantitative relation of one to the other, and still less the quantitative relation of one imagined lot to another lot, what then, I would ask, becomes of the 'calculus,' and, with it, of scientific Hedonism? And, secondly, to come to the first point, if it is not true that all pleasures can be compared as degrees of pleasantness, if the ideas of past pleasures are seldom exact copies of the reality, if they are too heterogeneous to be always compared, and if this holds *à fortiori* of pleasures in prospect; if, again, the changing mood of the subject conditions the quantity of pleasantness in a way not always to be calculated, then once more the 'calculus' is seen to be an impossibility.

It is unnecessary for me to enter on these objections, since partly they speak for themselves, and, in addition, I can refer to Mr. Sidgwick's book (pp. 120–130) for a discussion which in the main confirms them sufficiently. So that when we hear from him (Mind, V. p. 36) that 'we can perfectly well compare a pleasure felt under any given conditions with any other, however otherwise conditioned, and pronounce it equal or unequal; and we surely require no more than this to enable us to take "amount of pleasure" as our standard for deciding between alternatives of conduct,' we may content ourselves with remarking that his assertion is not only in direct contradiction with the facts of life, but is also irreconcileable with his own more sober views.

II. And, to come now to the second main head, the 'greatest sum of pleasures' is open to very serious objection.

(i) The cardinal point in my opinion is that the Good must be a whole, and that hence a mere aggregate is not the Good. The true End is not put together out of counted units, but the Hedonistic End is a mere addition of particulars. 'Irrelevant metaphysic' as any such consideration may be for our author, I hold it to be fatal to the greatest-pleasure doctrine in any form.

(ii) The next point is that, if by greatest sum we mean an infinite quantity, then that is a self-contradictory idea, which can indeed be aimed at, but by no possibility can be realised (vide Eth. Stud. pp. 70, 89).

(iii) Neither in his book nor in his article does our author tell us whether for him the sum is infinite or finite. A definition of happiness[1] (Methods, 19) points to the former view, but there is no certainty. If I knew that Mr. Sidgwick held to the infinite sum I would at once leave the matter here, remarking at the same time that he gives no hint of

---

[1] The definition of 'greatest happiness' on p. 109 tells us nothing. I think the reader will find (on such a minor point I will not burden him with references) that Mr. Sidgwick is somewhat wavering in his use of the term 'happiness.'

a solution of the problem of approximation to an endless sum.

But I do not suppose our author is prepared to say that the sum is infinite; and, though left in darkness, I must point out some difficulties which meet us when we take it as finite.

We may consider the sum either (a) as a series in time of units or groups of units, or (b) as a co-existing collection. I will take the series first.

(a) If a man is to have an end he can realize, then he must be able to say, It is mine, I possess it. And so with humanity, or the sentient creation generally; if there is a realizable end for them, there must be some time at which this end can be realized. But a sum of successive feelings is not such an end; for these pleasures do not exist as a sum, and to have the sum at any moment is impossible. Well but, I shall hear, is it not possible to go through the pleasures to the last, to sum the series, and to say, I have had them all? and have we not here an end which can be realized?

Taking first the case of the individual man, I answer, Yes doubtless, if you think that a man's end can be realized after he has ceased to be, and that it is enough that some one else, when he is dead, should say, He has summed the series, and attained the end. For myself I hold that a man's end is not realized at all unless during his existence, and that a good, which my whole life long I must be without, and which comes to me only with my extinction, is no good for me and not my good at all.

But Mr. Sidgwick does not hold *my* sum of pleasures to be the end. For him the end is the sum of the pleasures of the sentient creation, or, at the least, of humanity. But if this sum is a series in time I do not see how it ever is complete as a collection, so that any one can say humanity has realized the end by having had the sum, and I do not see who is to say it, and in fact I see only that I am using words which to me have no meaning [1].

---

[1] See more in Appendix, note A.

(*b*) Dismissing then the sum as a series, let us take it as a finite co-existing aggregate. Then the end will be that at any time the sentient world should be having the greatest possible quantity of pleasantness. In this case the realization of the *sum* lies open I think to no logical objection.

But *greatest possible* sum at once lands us in difficulties. What does it mean? When and in what sense can we say that I and the sentient world are having a greatest possible sum of pleasure?

I suppose the answer must be that the actual is that which under all the conditions was possible. One of these conditions is the direction of our energy towards increase of pleasure, and the total result (if the energy is so directed) we call the greatest possible sum, an end which can logically be realized wholly, and is really gained approximately. And I think, if it is clearly understood that we are dealing, not with an indefinite, but with a limited sum, that this answer so far may stand.

But if this is Mr. Sidgwick's answer, as perhaps it may be (I can only guess), yet, though it is true that not everything I have urged elsewhere (Eth. Stud. 89, and note) is applicable to our author, since he rejects the Hedonistic determination of the will, for all that we are by no means at the end of our difficulties.

The end is to get as much as we can. The realization of that is the *summum bonum*. If we suppose that at a given period of the world's history energy has been so far as was possible directed towards gaining pleasure, then the *summum bonum* is now realized, whatever the amount of the pleasure gained. Perfect virtue thus is and must be perfect happiness, and every failure to get perfect happiness is so much vice in oneself or others. An edifying conclusion, if reached by a somewhat strange road. But Hedonism, if it accepts this result, collides at once with ordinary notions of happiness. To say, If all had done and did their duty we should all be perfectly happy, no matter how small our surplus of pleasure —happiness at the next moment may be increased or diminished, but if all do their duty, the greatest possible sum of pleasures is at every moment realized, whatever be the fractional surplus of pleasure over pain—is surely a somewhat paradoxical assertion. But if we refuse to accept this hypothetical conclusion, then we fall back upon the unlimited quantity.

I have shown elsewhere (Eth. Stud. 95 note) that it will not help us if we take mere increase of pleasure as the end; and our result so far is that, even if the common Hedonistic psychology be dropped, and the end be taken neither as an infinite sum, nor as a successive series which must be summed before it is realized, we are in sharp collision with ordinary notions, though not at present in contradiction with ourselves.

But if we keep to Mr. Sidgwick, it seems to me that we shall have to contradict ourselves. He has not merely rejected the Hedonistic determination of the will, but has betaken himself to 'Freedom.' What he means by Free Will he has (as usual) not told us, yet, so far as we can see, in the sphere in which it holds, it is the same as pure chance.

If this is so we are at once in trouble. The realization of the greatest possible sum had a meaning when we could say, Here was a complex of conditions, concurring causes (or whatever else you like to call them), and this, which is actual, is the greatest possible result from that complex. The actual is what was possible. But when Free Will is brought in can we say this any longer? In the complication we are considering, acts of will are an element, and, if (as I understand our author does) you decline to say, This result which did follow *must* have followed, then you leave a reserve of possibility in the will, and the actual no longer is all that was possible. Hence greatest possible sum becomes a phrase without meaning. You never can say we have got that, because pure chance is admitted into the matter, and there is no telling that the wills of the agents might not, under all the conditions, have produced something else and something more; nor do I see how any exact limit can be put to the quantity of their action. Greatest possible actuality ceases in short to have a meaning when pure chance is once let in. It is a fiction, and a fiction is not an end which you can realize either wholly or, I think, approximately.

And here I will leave the subject. It would be an endless task to attempt to anticipate every sense in which the sum of pleasures can be taken, and it is probable that much of the above may be beside the mark. It is hard to discuss a man's opinions when you do not know what they are; and if our author has ever asked himself the meaning of 'the sum,' he has at present not imparted his answer to the public.

The questions which call for a discussion are these. Is the sum limited or unlimited? If limited, is it to be taken as a series or as a co-existing aggregate? If the latter, what is the exact meaning of greatest possible sum? If it is to be considered as a series, has not the series to be completed before it is realized? and, if so, when and how is it completed? Is the end mere approximation? and again, Can you be said to approximate to the impossible? Is once more the sum infinite? And, if it is so, is it not a fiction? No Hedonist, I think, can fairly refuse to enter on these questions; and then there remains the 'irrelevant' metaphysic, which I do not ask Mr. Sidgwick but do ask the reader to consider, Is not the end a whole, and, if so, can it be a mere collection or aggregate or series?

And now after this wearisome discussion, for the length of which I do not think that I am responsible, let us leave the criticism of 'greatest sum of pleasures' and try to see how this sum can be a 'real end of Reason.' We did not get very clear on Reason, and so must not wonder if this point too remains somewhat obscure. Does Reason give the mere abstraction of pleasure in general? Then pleasure of others and amount of pleasure both fall outside it. Does it give us the intuition of a collection of pleasures without reference to this or that subject, and is 'so great' or 'greatest' included in this intuition? That does seem a great deal to ask of Reason. And then is the intuition universal or individual? Does, once more, Reason not give the end at all but only qualify it? Is both 'pleasure' and 'sum of pleasures' given as the end apart from Reason, and does the latter merely add 'objective' to this ready-made end? Then, as we have said, the end is hardly the 'end of Reason.' Does, again, an intuition of Reason tell me that my greatest sum of pleasure is the end, but tell me at the same time that my end is 'objective' and the same for all subjects? Perhaps. I can not say.

But what is meant by the objectivity of the end? In one sense it is not 'objective,' because all pleasures are merely subjective. Nor in another sense is it objective, because it ought to be and therefore is not[1]. It seems to be objective in the following sense. We get somehow the notion of pleasure and greatest sum of pleasures as the end of our being, and, whether reason comes in or is there already, the result of reason is that the end is objective and right. And objective seems to mean this. Strip from sum of pleasures all reference to myself, and it ceases to be *my* pleasure. Strip from its pursuit all reference to any one in particular, and it is a pursuit for no one in particular, and that means (*how ?*) what is imperative on all alike. I can not venture to assert that this is our author's doctrine, and so will not risk a mistaken and wasted criticism. All I will say is that, *if* this is his doctrine, then 'objective[2]' means 'abstract,' and, with the abstraction from the desiring and willing individual, there is no more possibility of the objective being a goal to all, or imperative on any one. If it is not the end of any one in particular, then it is not the end in general or at all.

The question of the 'reasonable' as 'objective' will return on us when we try to understand Mr. Sidgwick's view of ethical science. But now we have partly realized the doubtful nature of our terms, and seen some of the psycho-

---

[1] There are some noticeable sayings on the opposition of 'ought' and 'is' on pp. 3, 92, 94. If Mr. Sidgwick had not qualified this statement on p. 5, he could hardly have avoided the conclusion, Nothing which is, ought to be, and might even be taken to hold, Whatever is not ought to be. I do not think this is a mere matter of verbal accuracy.

[2] I have been forced to ask myself the question what 'objective' means in the Methods of Ethics; but as it is not *necessary* for the reader to follow this enquiry, I have printed it in the Appendix (note B).

logical and metaphysical difficulties which beset our main thesis, it is time to ask what proof have we got that it is true? How are we to show that the greatest surplus of units of pleasantness is the end?

PART II.—THE ARGUMENT.

§ 5.—*The Intuition*[1].

We have seen what the Hedonistic end is, and we have now to prove that this is not merely *an* end but *the* end, that nothing else whatever is strictly speaking an end at all.

The method is simple. First, we show that nothing is ultimately good unless it enters into relation to consciousness of some kind. Then we separate what is left into 'objective' and 'subjective,' and finding the former is not the end, we lastly put the 'subjective' as the end and accept that.

Against the first step I have nothing to say, provided that consciousness is taken to mean (as we have seen it does mean) life, or mind in the widest sense. But against the rest of the proof I will make at once two preliminary objections.

(i) It must be shown (not asserted) that the alternative of objective and subjective is tenable. Failing this, the proof goes. (ii) It is a logical error to argue, Because A is not desirable without B, therefore B by itself is desirable; or again, Because A + B and B (by itself) are both desirable, therefore nothing but B is desirable. In other words however correct it is, having both A and B isolated, to say B is better than A, and A is not worth having, yet you cannot possibly go from that to, Therefore B is as good as A and B together, and B is the only good. We shall see the application of this directly.

To proceed. We accept the first proposition that consciousness (= life) is the end of life; but we at once demur to the alternative of subjective and objective. We say, first,

---

[1] Throughout this I presuppose in the reader an acquaintance with the chapter on the 'Summum Bonum.'

that this is a false alternative, and next, that it does not carry the required conclusion. What our author has to show is not merely that pleasure is *a* good or a *better* good, but that it is *the* good and the *only* good.

To the falseness of the alternative we shall return, but first of all we shall take the question (as we have a right to do), Apart from alternatives is pleasure for pleasure's sake the good? Is it even by itself good or desirable at all?

The appeal I understand to be 'to the intuitive judgment of each reader' (371) In what sense it is to his intuitive reason I hardly know.

We know what the Hedonistic end is. It is 'the sum of pleasures valued in proportion to their pleasantness.' It is in short Pleasantness as the one end, all else as means. And now I ask the reader to put this before himself as a moral agent, and say not Do I like it? but Is it the end of my being, the ultimate good, the real end of Reason? Is it for me and for others the one thing worth having for itself?

That I submit is the only fair way to put the issue. How does Mr. Sidgwick put it?

'But now, when we have so far limited the application of the notion Good to conscious life, it may seem that our result is really identical with what we call Happiness. For Happiness was explained to be preferable or desirable feeling or consciousness : and if we say that all other things called good are only means to the end of making conscious life intrinsically better or more desirable, is not this saying that they are means to the end of happiness ?' (369).

Now I think the reader will see why we spent so much time over 'desirable' and 'consciousness.' But it is not fair to Mr. Sidgwick to stop here. The passage goes on,

'On the other hand, it seems clear that in ordinary thought consciousness, active and passive, is conceived to be preferable on other grounds than its pleasantness.'

Our author now proceeds to the alternative we shall discuss hereafter, and puts the question, Are mere 'objects' desirable?

'But can this, on reflection, be maintained? It seems to me that it certainly cannot. Here I can only appeal to the intuitive judgment of each reader, when the question is fairly placed before it. For my own part, if I have any intuition at all respecting the ultimate ends of action, it seems to me that I can see this: that these objective relations of the conscious subject, when distinguished in reflective analysis from the consciousness accompanying and resulting from them, are not ultimately and intrinsically desirable: any more than material or other objects are, when considered out of relation to conscious existence altogether. Admitting that we have actual experience of such preferences as have just been described, of which the ultimate object is something that is not Feeling: it still seems to me that when such objects are conceived to come, not apparently or transiently, but really and finally, into competition with Happiness, we cannot maintain the rationality of such preferences' (371-2).

All I shall say at present on this passage is that it plainly does not carry the required conclusion, i.e. 'a mere pursuit of universal happiness.' Admit every word of it, and yet it gives us no right to say the end is nothing but the subjective. Better does not=the only thing good. Nor again by showing that an element by itself is not *the* end or *an* end can you prove that it is *nothing but* a means.

After accounting for the aversion 'we find in Common Sense' 'to admit Happiness (when explained to mean a sum of pleasures) to be the sole ultimate end and standard of right conduct;' and after again defining Pleasure as 'Preferable or Desirable Feeling of whatever kind' (372), where the reader will not forget the ambiguity of the terms, the Hedonistic end is once more presented to us for our acceptance.

'But Universal Happiness, desirable conscious life for the innumerable multitude of living beings, present and to come, seems an End that satisfies our imagination by its vastness, and sustains our resolution by its comparative permanence and security.'

I am very far from accusing Mr. Sidgwick of intentional unfairness. But I must leave it to the reader to judge whether this is the right way to put the question. The ambiguity (for a time removed), as at the beginning (369), so now at the end wraps the issue in a cloud. No one, I am

sure, who himself kept the problem in view could state it
in such a way; and the crowning phrase 'desirable conscious
life' combines *petitio principii* with *ignoratio elenchi* after
a manner not easy to parallel. The thesis to be proved is
that mere pleasure is the end. Mr. Sidgwick writes conscious life for pleasure, and adds desirable (which *means* end)
to the definition.

Whether our author feels secure in the position which so
far he has taken I can hardly tell. At all events he does
not remain there, but moves to what he evidently considers
the decisive point.

'If we simplify the question by supposing only a single sentient
conscious being in the universe, it then is surely evident that
nothing can be ultimately 'good' for such a being except his own
happiness.' (374; cf. 378, 360, 392 note.)

Mr. Sidgwick, as I understand, appeals here to 'Common
Sense,' and I am quite ready to go before that tribunal; but
first there are one or two questions to be asked. *Can* we so
'simplify the question?' Have we a *right* so to simplify it?
And on our author's theory *do* we simplify it so?

(i) The supposition of one finite conscious being in a material universe, which Mr. Sidgwick introduces so modestly, is
an utter impossibility, not only according to at least one half
of philosophical theory, but also according to current religious
belief.

(ii) It is simple dogmatic individualism to assume that
the end for all is the mere multiple of the end for one, which
therefore can be found by isolating an unit. Here again we
must say that an author has a right to make what assumptions he pleases, but surely not to introduce them tacitly.

(iii) The supposition is so far from simplifying the question that it at once involves Mr. Sidgwick in contradiction
with himself. The words 'ultimately and intrinsically good
or desirable' (392, note) mean the same as 'objectively good'
or 'reasonable.' But this was valid not for one individual as
such, but was 'the same for all minds.' Is it not then a contradiction, given but one conscious individual, that his end

should be objective? But, if not objective, then not ultimately good.

But if this does not hold, and if one individual may consider *his* pleasure to be objectively desirable, then the argument against egoism (see below) will be shaken if not destroyed [1].

The only way that I see out of this dilemma is to suppose the single sentient to have an intuition of Reason, which tells him that pleasure in general, or in the abstract, is the end of his being: whereon he proceeds dutifully to pursue *his own* pleasure simply for the sake of pleasure in general. But I do not understand Mr. Sidgwick to maintain this.

Now I think if we pleased we should after this have a right to refuse to go before 'Common Sense' with Mr. Sidgwick's supposition. Nevertheless we will not refuse. Figure yourself then, reader—your imagination, not like mine, may keep pace with our author's—figure yourself as a single sentient being in a non-sentient universe, and tell us, would you not believe in 'a real end of Reason, the absolutely Good or Desirable?' Would you not say, I can reach my end; there *is* something I *ought* to live for, and that is my pleasure?

The reader must answer the question, for I confess my fancy is too weak to realize the position. So far as I can do so, I answer it in the negative.

And now that we have put the Hedonistic end, let us look at the alternative, the true alternative, which involves no 'hypothesis unverifiable by experience.' But we must come to this through two one-sided statements of the issue :—

(i) Let us first understand by the 'objective' end something out of relation to the mind. Is this the end? I think we may say it is not.

(ii) Next let us suppose (I think this is what Mr. Sidgwick means) certain relations of our wills to other wills, or more generally, certain relations of our minds to something not

---

[1] Notice on p. 374 the wavering view of the reasonable, according to which one's 'own happiness seems to be a rational ultimate end.' This will meet us again.

our minds (371, 375), and this in entire abstraction from pleasure. Let us distinguish these 'in reflective analysis' from all feeling, and ask, Is function, apart from pleasure, a human end?

Elsewhere I said Yes to this question. I think that was rash. I can say neither Yes nor No, for I am sure now that I cannot perform the analysis required so as to bring the residuum before me practically. When I try to think what I should be like without pleasure or pain, I can find no certain result. Abstracting from these, I find the relation of my will to the universal will to be so unreal an abstraction that the words mean nothing at all, or, at least, nothing practical. I must leave the reader to answer the question for himself; and, so far as my views are concerned, he is most welcome to answer it in the negative [1].

---

[1] In Mind (V. 36) Mr. Sidgwick says, 'He (the Hedonist) is only concerned to maintain that, when in a mood of calm reflection we distinguish these ideal objects (such as the pursuit of truth, &c.) from the feelings inseparably connected with them, it is the quality of these latter which we see to be the ultimate end of rational desire.' The passage illustrates well our author's loose terminology. It is much the same statement as we quoted on p. 27 from Methods 371-2. There we had 'consciousness,' and here 'quality of feelings.' I will try to define the issue.

(1) Does Mr. Sidgwick mean by *quality of feelings* the mere pleasantness of them, entirely distinct from every other quality they possess? If not, his conclusion disappears.

(2) Does he mean that in the pursuit of truth, &c., we can distinguish, first the feelings from the activities, and then, next, the pleasantness of the feelings from their other qualities, and bring these things severally before our minds as distinct objects of choice? If not, once more his conclusion vanishes.

For that conclusion it is necessary that, taking the idea (e.g.) of the pursuit of truth, I should be able to separate in my mind, first, the feelings from the activities, and, next, the bare pleasantness of the feelings from every other quality they have, in such a way as to be able to contemplate, as several objects, first this mere pleasantness, and then the residue of feeling and activity; and to be able to say the element of pleasantness is the one end, and all the rest is not an end at all, nor goes to make the end an end, but is a bare means or accompaniment.

I do not believe that any one can perform this operation: and for myself, so far as I can make any approach to such a choice, it does not appear to me that the pleasantness, in its abstraction, is even *an* end. Still less does it appear that it is *the* end, and that all the rest of the feeling and activity is a bare accompaniment or means. But the reader must judge for himself.

The alleged fact that we can compare all pleasant things in respect of the

But there is another way of putting it which I think *is* intelligible. Given maintenance or heightening of function on one side with the same or less pleasure: given on the other side lowering of function in qualitative excellence (I have said elsewhere what I mean by these words) with the same or more pleasure—which is your end? not, Which would you like best, but Which *ought* you to take? Given even (for argument's sake) the possibility or certainty that what we call progress might entail, not mere loss of pleasure, but actually a less amount of pleasure than pain to the creation or to humanity—which is the *right* course? Hedonism tells us (this follows from p. 384) that progress is here an absolute evil, because the surplus counts and the surplus is pain. The issue, I think, is fair and tolerably intelligible, and I will leave it to the reader. Hedonism falls if the question is answered in the way I answer it[1].

(iii) But I deny the right of any one to compel us to such a choice, unless he first proves against us what Mr. Sidgwick does not attempt to prove, nor even asserts. We do not separate 'objective' and 'subjective:' we do not say, Virtue *or* pleasure, and Pleasure *or* virtue: we say *both*. The true issue is virtue + pleasure as the end, against mere pleasure as the end. To say, Function is the end, is by no means to say, Pleasure is not good. It is to say, Pleasure is an inseparable element in the human end, and in that sense is necessarily included in the end; and higher life implies pleasure for the reason that life without pleasure is inconceivable. What we hold to against every possible modification of Hedonism is that the standard and test is in higher and lower function, not in more or less pleasure. *If* any one can prove that higher life means less or no surplus of pleasure, *then* he can fairly ask us to face the alternative. We are

---

amount of their pleasantness, does not show (as Mr. Sidgwick to seems think it does) that we can put bare pleasantness on one side, and everything else on the other, and, bringing these as several objects before the mind, make our choice between them. And besides, the alleged fact is contrary to experience (see above, p. 18).

[1] In the passage quoted from Mind, V. 36, Mr. Sidgwick appears to deny this; but I may not understand him rightly.

ready to do this, but against Mr. Sidgwick we certainly need not do so unless we please.

I have been forced to repeat a good deal of that which I have said elsewhere: it would be little more than a similar repetition did I enter on the remaining difficulties of the chapter; and as Mr. Sidgwick (in his article on Hedonism, Mind, V.) brought forward nothing against the doctrine I advanced, I must consider that it stands. The result of this section, in my judgment, is, that our author has not shown the greatest surplus of pleasure to be *the* end, nor even an end at all.

§ 6.—*Unconscious Hedonism.*

The latter part of the foregoing section has, I think, removed by anticipation the argument from the latent or unconscious Hedonism of common morality. Indeed, as an independent proof this seems to have no weight at all. To go through the virtues and to show that they all bring pleasure establishes the thesis, Virtue in general is pleasant, and it establishes no more. To conclude from Virtue is pleasant, to Pleasure is the end and virtue merely the means, is surely a logical leap of some width. If you could show (and Mr. Sidgwick has not done so) that the greatest surplus of pleasure comes from what we call virtue, i.e. that no other way of life we call not-virtuous could have produced a greater, even then you have not proved one step towards the Hedonistic thesis. The argument may hold against asceticism; that is for the ascetic to dispute. Against us it does not hold. If the end is the fullest life for each with the most harmonious life for all, the most harmonious life for each with the fullest life for all, it is not very hard to see why virtue should in general be pleasant, nor need it stagger us to be told (though neither we nor Mr. Sidgwick affirm this) that what we call the most virtuous life is, when the whole is considered, also the most pleasant. I am unable to see how, if this is so, it goes to show either that one element of the whole is the end and the other nothing but a means, or even that the element of pleasure is to be used as the criterion for the element of virtue. The reason for placing the criterion in function rather than pleasure (even on the hypothesis that greatest pleasure must coincide on the whole with highest function) is that the function is definite and the pleasure indefinite. I have stated these points elsewhere, and Mr. Sidgwick has advanced nothing against them.

§ 7.—*The Suppression of Egoism.*

We come now to one of the most characteristic parts of the Methods of Ethics. It is always interesting to study the position of the Hedonist towards Egoism, particularly to those who, like myself, feel sure that consistent Hedonism must be egoistic. We will first see what Mr. Sidgwick's attitude towards Egoism is, and then try to understand the reason of it.

Our author's Egoist is the man who pursues the maximum of his own pleasure; and since, as we have seen, right and wrong are 'objective,' and reason apprehends the universal, it is natural to think that for Mr. Sidgwick it would have been plain at once that egoism and morality are irreconcileable, and that to show this by 'argument' was not only superfluous but impossible.

No doubt there is a method of arguing with the Egoist in the sense of the man who takes his self for his end. Argument is possible as to the nature of the self; and the Egoist may be convinced perhaps that he has made a mistake. But in Mr. Sidgwick we find no hint of the kind, and indeed anything of the sort would be for him, I suppose, an 'hypothesis unverifiable by experience.'

Failing this, I should have said the only course left was to call attention to the immorality and 'irrationality' of Egoism, and so leave it. Mr. Sidgwick does not do this: he approaches the Egoist with 'argument' (391, 392, note) or 'proof' (461). And in this 'argument,' which I have done my best to understand, I can see no more than one or two tautologies.

D

We have first two 'self-evident truths,' of which each seems to be 'an indubitable intuition of the practical Reason' (371 ; cf. 470). These are the Rule of Equity and the Rule of Benevolence.

The first is ' " Whatever I judge reasonable or unreasonable that another should do for me : that by the same judgment I declare reasonable or unreasonable that I should *in the like case* do for him " ' (358).

With all due respect for our author's opinion, this Rule seems to me to be a pure tautology. The right, the objective, the reasonable, is, by the definition, what holds in abstraction from ' the mere fact that I and he are different individuals' (358), or 'the mere individuality of different individuals' (183, note), or again 'the mere fact that *he is he*' (391). The meaning of 'reasonable' is what holds in abstraction from the individual, and hence is the same in all individuals. If we really wish to be 'reasonable' we must write X for 'me' and 'him,' these being unreasonable distinctions, and then the Rule is, Whatever X judges reasonable or unreasonable that X should do for X : that by the same judgment X declares reasonable or unreasonable that X should *in the like case* do for X. That, as soon as we know that reasonable = universal, is surely a bare tautology.

The second Rule, without any doubt 'an indubitable intuition of the practical Reason' (371 ; cf. 468, 470, 472), is the Rule of Benevolence.

'Here we are supposed to judge that there is something intrinsically desirable—some result which it would be reasonable for each individual to seek for himself if he considered himself alone. Let us call this the individual's Good or Welfare : then what Clarke urges is, that the Good of any one individual cannot be *more* intrinsically desirable, *because it is his*, than the equal Good of any other individual.' (360.)

'I cannot regard the fulfilment of my desires, or my own happiness, as intrinsically more desirable (or more to be regarded by me as a rational end) than the equal happiness of any one else.' (364.)

Mr. Sidgwick proceeds :

'But now, of these two propositions, the first is a necessary postulate of *all* ethical systems, being an expression of what is involved in the mere conception of objective rightness and wrongness of conduct, while the second is the fundamental principle of that particular system which (in Book I.) we called Utilitarianism.'

The first of these propositions, I remark, is not an expression of what is involved but of what is explicitly stated in 'objective rightness;' and here again in the second the phrases 'desirable' and 'rational end' postulate abstraction from 'the individuality of the individual.' In respect of the rules we have no right to distinguish one individual from another, and this second proposition comes to no more than 'X cannot regard his own happiness as more desirable than the equal happiness of X,' which seems to me either tautological or nonsensical [1].

As Mr. Sidgwick says, 'This seems to be as much a self-evident truth as the principle of Equity' (360). I agree with him in this point. My objection is that it is *self*-evident in the sense of having the self-same subject and predicate, and that, in short, in a different form it is the tautology we had before [2].

We think then that our author not only 'may seem to have laboriously executed one of those circles in reasoning before noticed' (366), but certainly has done so: and when he proceeds, 'We seem to have done nothing: and in fact we have only evolved the suppression of Egoism, the necessary universality of view, which is implied in the mere form of the objective judgment "that an end is good," just as it is in the

---

[1] In plain words, these rules are, What is good for X is good for X, and what is right for X is right for X. They cannot mean, What is good and right for *one* X is so for *another* and a *different* X. Right and good are the same for each, and each is the same for right and good. The 'difference' Mr. Sidgwick supposes to be constituted by 'individuality' falls outside the 'universal' and 'objective.' In saying 'reasonable' we postulate indifference to 'the individuality of the individuals,' and hence the words 'one' and 'other' are irrelevant. By introducing them you mean to add nothing to the universal at all, or, if you do, you flatly contradict our author's view of 'objective rightness.'

[2] It ceases to be a tautology only if it postulates absolutely that pleasure is *an* end or *the* end. Then it becomes a mere assumption and, if any argument is meant, a glaring *petitio*. But I do not understand Mr. Sidgwick to put it forward in the above sense.

judgment "that an action is right"'—it is impossible for us not to answer, You really have done nothing, and have 'evolved' nothing but that which long ago you explicitly postulated.

So far our only way with the Egoist has been to reiterate the postulates which he denies, and if the argument is to proceed we must do more. We must make him accept them, and on paper it is but to ask and to have. The Egoistic Hedonist, who holds that absolutely nothing but his subjective pleasure is the end, advances 'the proposition that his happiness or pleasure is objectively desirable' (391), and having thus admitted that his own doctrine is false, naturally is at once confuted and ignominiously suppressed.

It is hard to discuss this matter with gravity. I will merely remark that the egoistic Hedonist who could admit the above proposition would show that he simply did not know what he was saying. 'Objectively desirable' means desirable *not* for me in particular, and the Hedonistic egoist is the man he is by holding that *nothing* is 'objectively desirable.'

He would laugh if you said to him of his happiness that 'the mere fact (if I may so put it) that *he is he* can have nothing to do with its objective desirability or goodness' (391). 'I pursue my pleasure, my dear Sir, not because I am I, nor for the sake of any other tautology, but because I feel it and like it, while yours I can neither feel nor like.' Would not this be his answer to our author's 'argument'? And Mr. Sidgwick fully admits that argument is here of no avail (391) [1].

---

[1] But even here he makes the Egoist say 'that he ought to take his own happiness or pleasure as his ultimate end.' This too is surely inaccurate. 'Ought' for Hedonistic egoism refers only to the means. Cf. Ethical Studies, p. 116. On the whole subject of Egoism, as treated by Mr. Sidgwick, I have failed to find a consistent view. He not only (374) allows that Egoism is reasonable, but on p. 391, when he formulates the Egoistic first principle in two ways, and says that against the second the 'proof' holds, while against the first (as just quoted) it does not, I cannot see the vital distinction. If 'ought'='reasonable' (80, note), and 'right'='reasonable,' and is 'the same, whether recognised or not, for all Minds or Subjects' (182), surely the moment the Egoist says he *ought* to take the end he does, he contradicts himself, and

But let us turn to the more interesting question, what has led our author into this position against Egoistic Hedonism. The answer is in a word that Mr. Sidgwick dares not break entirely with this view for fear his own ground should give way beneath him. He not only, as we shall see hereafter, has doubts whether Egoism be not 'reasonable;' but, if his own thesis is to stand, it is of the last importance that Egoistic Hedonism should *not* be suppressed wholly. His tactics (I use the word in no offensive sense) are, standing on Egoistic Hedonism to universalize that into Utilitarianism. Of *my pleasure* he wants to keep one part (pleasure) and drop only the *my*. And to do this the Egoist must be won over— hence the 'argument.' But even if the Egoist become an ally, I think this movement cannot be executed in the face of an enemy. What it comes to is, as I have said elsewhere, Take from Egoistic Hedonism pleasure as the end, take from morality the 'universal' and the 'reasonable,' and then argue, *My* pleasure is not a reasonable end, pleasure in general is not mine, therefore pleasure in general is a reasonable end. This of course is futile; and the only way left to separate the 'my' from 'pleasure' is to postulate in a single sentient an intuition of my pleasure as pleasure in general, which seems to be an untenable position (I cannot say if it is our author's). It naturally leads to the doctrine that the 'my' and 'your' are an illusion, and that mine when viewed under the light of reason is the same as yours [1]. This result (substantially

the proof holds just as much as when he says 'his happiness or pleasure is objectively desirable or good.' Where is the difference?

[1] The reader will find it instructive here to develope a doctrine of non-hedonistic Egoism. Suppose the law of the universe by which it progresses to be the struggle for existence, the reckless self-assertion of each against all. Suppose that the individuals are aware of this law, then is it not both the 'objective' and 'subjective' end of the individual to assert himself against all to the uttermost? By making himself his sole end, is he not fulfilling the objective end, the intrinsically desirable, &c.? Against this position (not mine) what form would Mr. Sidgwick's 'reasonable' take? The fact that I am I, if I have most force, is a vital difference to the end of the universe, and to get that end by getting the strongest to the front, there is (ex hypoth.) but one course, that we should struggle recklessly. I do not know whether any enthusiastic follower of Mr. Darwin has clearly developed this view. It is much to be wished that some one would. If the reader will carry it out for

the same as Schopenhauer's) could I think be deduced from our author's doctrine of the 'reasonable,' but, apart from the objections we entertain to the premises, the strict result would seem to be that not only the differences of 'you' and 'me' are illusory because irrational, but that also, and on the same ground, pain and pleasure are both illusions.

In our last section we shall come once more upon Egoism, but now we must turn to Mr. Sidgwick's view of Ethical Science, which seems vitally connected with his doctrine of Reason.

PART III.

§ 8.—*Mr. Sidgwick's view of Ethical Science.*

Ethical science does not yet exist; but it is possible. What is its nature? The end we know. The study of the means to the end is Eudemonics. This plus 'the acceptance of the end as absolutely prescribed' is Ethics (8). It treats of the ideal to be realized and the actions which are to realize it. Hence 'its affirmations are also precepts' (2, 3).

'The science of Ethics, therefore, necessarily treats of action which to a great extent is not : action therefore which (we may say) *ought* to be [1]. Its affirmations are also precepts : indeed, if it were not so, the distinction just drawn between Ethics and Psychology would vanish.' (3.)

The end, as was said before, we know. The means are the actions of men.

The object or scope of the 'science' is practical. It is to direct us to 'externally and objectively right' conduct (381). It is to tell us what to do, not merely in general, but in particular. It is to be no mere outline but a scientific code.

'For instinct varies and is uncertain, and sometimes gives no clear guidance at all : and yet we are convinced that the right

himself and bring it into collision with our author's 'argument' against Egoism, I think he will find that it throws light on the subject.

[1] We have already noticed that this view of 'ought' is open to serious criticism. A minor point would be the question whether 'science' is the proper term to use.

course must be the same for all, and ought to be determined upon universal principles; and it is for these that men appeal to the moralist.' (217.)

'Its aim is rather to shew a natural transition from the Morality of Common Sense to Utilitarianism, somewhat like the transition in special branches of practice from trained instinct and empirical rules to the technical method that embodies and applies the conclusions of science: so that Utilitarianism may appear only as the scientifically complete and systematically reflective form of that regulation of conduct, which through the whole course of human history has always tended in the same direction' (396) 'In the more technical parts of practice we prefer the judgment of a few trained experts to the instincts of the vulgar.' (434.)

In one word we are to have a system of Casuistry.

'For if the particular can be satisfactorily settled by conscience without reference to general rules, "Casuistry," which consists in the application of general rules to particular cases, is clearly superfluous. But then, on this view, we shall have no práctical need of any such general rules, or of a science of Ethics at all' (85; cf 295, *sub fin.*). And 'we study Ethics . . . for the sake of Practice.' (191.)

May the rules of this system collide? Certainly not.

'In order to have a complete theory of Ethics, we require not only to make our maxims perfectly precise, but also to systematize them completely, in order that no collision of precepts may remain possible.' (200.) 'Such a collision is absolute proof that at least one of the formulae needs qualification.' (320.) 'In conclusion, then, we must admit that while we find a number of broad and more or less indefinite rules unhesitatingly laid down by Common Sense in this department of duty; it is difficult or impossible to state even the most certain of these with such clearness and precision as would enable us to determine exactly the extent of duty in any case. And yet, as we saw, such exactness seems to be required for the perfection of practice no less than for theoretical completeness, in so far as those duties are liable to come into apparent conflict with each other, and with other prescriptions of the moral code.' (235, cf. 388.)

For an act to be right we see it must come under one head or clause of the code, and that this cannot be at variance with any other.

'One may hold that duty varies with the individual and is so far relative, and yet maintain that it varies on rational grounds, capable of being explained, systematized, and reduced to principles.' (6; cf. 377 *sub fin.*)

Briefly then we see Mr. Sidgwick's conception of Ethics is wholly jural.

It is at this point that an interesting question, the relation of morality to law, is opened. My knowledge of the subject, I am sorry to say, even did space permit, would not enable me to enter on it. I do not know how far, as a matter of fact, any code of law can be made so systematic as not to contradict itself. But there are two obvious points which present themselves here. First, no modern code makes the smallest attempt to regulate our whole life in accordance with a leading principle. And secondly, a most important point, all law abstracts and must abstract, while morality may not do so. In morals we take a case and we ask, Is this morally right or wrong and how far? Here we can refuse to consider no single item of the whole complication. The previous life of the man, his difference from other men, the combination of circumstances in its general character and then in its relation to *this* man, all have to be admitted in a moral judgment. You cannot say 'such and such an act is wrong, and wrong to such an extent,' and then bring the man under the law as such and such a case of criminality. But, on the other hand, is not law obliged to do this? Is it not from its very nature compelled to keep to the 'universal' and to treat the whole case as an abstraction, i.e. as a *mere* instance of the law, which the case really *never* is. Is not the best administered and best law possible compelled either to leave such liberty to the administrator that practically it ceases to be law, or else obliged seldom quite to coincide with morality, and too often to come into a collision with it, which, though unavoidable, is none the less painful[1]? I submit these questions to the judgment of

---

[1] I do not mean that Law can never try to judge the whole case morally; but I think I am right in supposing that it does not do so except in considering the amount of punishment, and again of damages in civil (are they really civil?) actions of a certain sort.

the reader, and if we are obliged to answer them in the affirmative, then I would put one more question, Does not this nature of law raise a strong presumption against the jural view of Ethics?

Turning now to the question of a moral code we see an alternative awaits us. Either you are prepared to give up your code at a certain point, or else you must attempt to get every possible complication within its clauses.

To accept the former is to throw the code over. Ethics is no longer 'a complete method for determining right conduct' (217). Our judgment is no more 'a systematic deduction from rules' (85). And even then we are left with the question, Do not the rules collide? The opinion which I have put forward elsewhere is that they both do and must.

But I understand our author to accept the second proposition. All complications, I understand him to say, are to be anticipated in the code, or at least so provided for there that the act will come without collision under some one head[1].

What we are going to try to show is that this attempt to get every qualification inside the code leaves in the end *nothing* outside, so that the objective criterion becomes merely subjective, and will justify *any* action whatever. In short, just as in metaphysic we see abstract individualism and abstract universalism turn round the one into the other, just as in Kant's Practical Philosophy the categorical imperative covered in the end anything or nothing, so in our author's Hedonistic casuistry we shall find that 'objective rightness,' just because he has made it *so* objective, becomes in fact merely subjective. It is an old story that extremes meet, and Mr. Sidgwick has illustrated it once more.

'One may hold that duty varies with the individual and is so

---

[1] The teaching that we should act sometimes on impulse, the 'self-limiting' power of Reason (323-4), together with what is said as to tact (202, cf. 206), merely means, I think, that we in our practice may find the clause best sometimes by not thinking of it. That the *moralist* not only may, but must, draw his code so as to exhibit every right act as a deduction from it, will be seen from the passages quoted and referred to above to be Mr. Sidgwick's doctrine.

far relative, and yet maintain that it varies on rational grounds, capable of being explained, systematized, and reduced to principles. So much relativity, indeed, is admitted to some extent in all moral systems. But if it be maintained that two men may act in two different ways under circumstances precisely similar, and yet neither be wrong because each thinks himself right: then the common notion of morality must be rejected as a chimera. That there is in any given circumstances some one thing which ought to be done and that this can be known, is a fundamental assumption, made not by philosophers only, but by all men who perform any processes of moral reasoning.' (6.)

That there is some *one* thing right is false, if ever in any circumstances there can be two courses *either* of which is right. Certainly common opinion holds that this is possible, and how on Mr. Sidgwick's view it is impossible that two courses might equally conduce to the greatest surplus I cannot see. But if this is so, then the proposition 'that two men' &c. must be reconsidered.

This is not perhaps an important point, but it is as well not to set down at the beginning an inaccurate statement as a 'fundamental assumption.'

To proceed, at all events 'Right and Wrong are really objective: that is, the same, whether recognised or not, for all Minds or Subjects' (182–3). But what does this mean? That what is right for you must be right for me? No.

'If then I assert any action to be right, I imply that it would be right for any other person in my circumstances : or (for obviously that the circumstances are *my* circumstances cannot make it right) for all persons in precisely similar circumstances.' (183.)

This sounds well ; and, hearing further 'that the rightness at any rate of most actions is altered by a *material* alteration of circumstances,' we naturally now want to know what circumstances may be 'material.' Some of these we shall see hereafter, but we find a decided answer to the general question in the note to the above page.

'It should be observed that difference of circumstances must be taken to include difference of nature and character—in short all differences beyond the mere individuality of different individuals.'

So much is certain. But what is 'the mere individuality of different individuals?' Ah, that is the sort of question no modest enquirer tries to answer. We keep to experience, and use these categories so far as for his practical purposes every one must. To ask what they mean, what *we* mean when we use them, would it not be to discuss 'hypotheses unverifiable by experience?' Indeed, in too many cases I think so; or shall we say, not 'unverifiable by experience,' but there most verifiable as the fictions of a onesided theory?

We must take it, I suppose, that this 'mere individuality' is what you have left after you have got a variety of men and abstracted all the differences of nature and character. The residue of myself, after my nature and character are removed, is my individuality.

Let us take it so. But then the result which *must* follow is that everything beside this residuum is objective. The circumstances of nature and character will *not* be '*my* circumstances.' They will be material to and will qualify rightness, and rightness is objective. The act is right because it is an instance deducible from the code. We have seen the extent of the circumstances which may enter into the act, and it is now obvious that *either* we must give up the idea of deciding right and wrong systematically from a code, *or* we must provide in the code for all these complications, not only for all combinations of outward events, but also for the differences of nature and character. Otherwise we shall have only a 'subjective criterion.'

It is much to be wished that Mr. Sidgwick would express himself more definitely on this point. As it is, I cannot understand him to do anything but accept the second proposition. Let us proceed, however, to the practical application of the code.[1]

'We must observe that the admission of an exception on general grounds is merely the establishment of a more complex and delicate rule, instead of one that is broader and simpler: for if it is

---

[1] I must earnestly beg the reader to go through the whole chapter, Bk. iv. c. 5, not only to check me, but to convince himself.

conducive to the general good that the exception be admitted in one case, it will be equally so in all similar cases.' (448.)

We see so far that 'exceptions on general grounds' are allowable, since they are not really exceptions at all, but additions to the code. How simple and how workable that code will be the reader may stop to consider. Or rather let him wait until he has read the following :—

'There is, however, another kind of exceptions, differing fundamentally from this, which Utilitarianism seems to admit : where the agent does not think it expedient that the rule on which he himself acts should be *universally* adopted, and yet maintains that his individual act is right, as producing a greater balance of pleasure over pain than any other conduct open to him would produce.' (449.)

Here most persons would have thought is an end of the code altogether. But no,—

'Here, however, we seem brought into conflict with Kant's fundamental principle, that a right action must be one which the agent could desire to be done by all persons under similar circumstances : and yet it was argued (Book iii. c. 1, and c. 13), that this was a necessary truth involved in the very idea of right conduct. And it certainly seems to me such : only (as was noticed in Book iii. c. 7, in the particular case of veracity,) we must admit a qualification of this rule, which importantly modifies its practical application : we must include among relevant "circumstances" the belief (supposing it to exist) that the action will not be widely imitated. In short, the Kantian principle means no more than that no act can be right for me "because I am I :" if right for me, it must be right on general grounds and therefore for some class of persons : but there is no reason why this class should not be defined by the above-mentioned characteristic of believing that the act will remain an exceptional one.' (450.)

We are not surprised after this to find that—

'The Romanist view of the economy to be observed in the distribution of truth, seems to be strictly in harmony with Utilitarian principles.' (452.)

And, to continue the quotation :—

'So again, in so far as the harm of an act consists chiefly in its bad example, it may on Utilitarian principles be right if it can be done with perfect secresy, but not otherwise. On both these points Utilitarianism is manifestly at issue with Common Sense: for the very notion of the latter involves the repudiation of an esoteric morality, differing from that popularly taught: and an action which would be bad if done openly is not commonly thought to be rendered good by secresy.' (*ibid.*)

'Thus the Utilitarian conclusion, carefully stated, would seem to be this: that the opinion that secresy may render an action right which would not otherwise be so, should itself be kept comparatively secret: and similarly it seems expedient that the doctrine that esoteric morality is expedient should itself be kept esoteric.' (452-3.)

I suppose all this is to be inserted in the code, and at this point I will put it to the reader whether what it comes to is not in plain language this, that taking the greatest surplus of pleasure to the creation as the end, you may and ought to use your private judgment as to the means: that *any* act, no matter how seemingly immoral, is moral for you if you have a sincere opinion that it will increase the surplus. I will use no illustrations to help the reader to understand this doctrine; but I will venture so far as to ask him to make them for himself.

All that is left of the 'system of objective rules' is this. Having judged an act to be the means to the greatest pleasure, you add to your judgment the superfluous, if not senseless, formula, And if any one else were I, it would be right for him to judge and act as I do. Then you may call the act Right and Duty, or (perhaps) even more than Duty (456). If this is so, and follows necessarily from Mr. Sidgwick's teaching, then it may be no more than an idle fancy that once and again has made us think of the Probable Opinion; it may be wholly unfair to see the doctrine that the moralist tells men what they ought to think (352), and that Ethics is practical Casuistry, take the practical form of the Spiritual Director; but I think it is fair to say that Utilitarianism when carried out comes to something not unlike Jesuitry.

I have no reason to suppose Mr. Sidgwick to be more friendly to that cause than I am. But what he teaches, and what must follow from his teaching, we must take on its own merits. And at this point he may say he is treated unfairly, that these casuistical doctrines are valid only in the present transitory stage, where the morality of 'common sense' still lingers, and where the moralist has not yet (with the assistance of the sociologist) succeeded in constructing the full code. But I do not think this is what he means. Let us go on to the next paragraph.

'Of course in an ideal community of enlightened Utilitarians this swarm of puzzles and paradoxes would vanish : as in such a society no one can have any ground for believing that persons in circumstances similar to his own will act in a manner different to that which he adopts.' (453.)

Now I think we have a right to suppose that our author must maintain one of these two things. *Either* he holds that a time is coming, or may come, when the means leading to the maximum of pleasure will have been systematized with all the above qualifications in one harmonious code, and further believes that the community will be so enlightened as not merely to have mastered this code, but to be able by private judgment to bring each action under the fitting clause—*or* he does not affirm this, but thinks that the relative distinction of the 'enlightened' and 'the vulgar' may or must continue.

If he accepts the first alternative I withdraw my objections. But I shall leave it to the reader to judge whether argument is any longer possible; whether we are not in the realm of fiction and apocalyptic literature; whether, after having emptied the contents of each human being into this monstrous code, Mr. Sidgwick has not been forced to postulate something like omniscience in 'the individuality of the individuals' which is left to execute it.

But if he accepts the second then does not all that I have urged hold good? When we look things in the face, is it not moral for any one, who likes to call himself a moralist, to use and act on his private judgment as to the means which will produce the maximum of pleasure in any and every case in which he chooses to do so? And has not so far the result proved mere individualism, and the objective criterion turned out 'subjective?'

'Ah but,' I may hear, 'Mr. Sidgwick distinguishes objective and subjective Rightness. Have you forgotten that?' Indeed I almost had. But let us see what 'objective rightness' means.

'By Utilitarianism is here meant the ethical theory, first distinctly formulated by Bentham, that the conduct which under any given circumstances is externally or objectively right, is that which will produce the greatest amount of happiness to all whose interests are affected.' (381.)

The end is the maximum surplus. The means are the actions and rules which necessarily lead to that end, according to Mr. Sidgwick in *one* way, but for argument's sake let us say in one or more possible ways. In any given circumstances there is one course of conduct (or several courses) which are externally and objectively right. And now I ask, How can this course be known? The science of Ethics does not exist; what can take its place? The science of Ethics, I make bold to say, while man is man *can* never exist. Even if the world never altered, to have a complete knowledge of the laws of life, and to be able to judge correctly the enormous complication of detail so as to say, This act will increase the surplus and that act will not—goes beyond the human knowledge that we find in experience. And if the world alters, then the idea of knowing beforehand the laws of that alteration and of calculating existing data accordingly, is the mere dream of a doctrinaire which omniscience alone could make real.

'That there is in any given circumstances some one thing which ought to be done, and that this can be known, is a fundamental assumption' (6). But if that thing be 'objective rightness' it cannot be known. To say of past conduct, This *was* objectively right, is to say, No other course would have produced more pleasure on the whole. To say of present conduct, This *is* objectively right, is to say no other course will produce a greater surplus of pleasure to humanity or the creation. Such knowledge seems to me so plainly beyond the reach of our minds that I think it is not worth while to dwell on the point. Once more I must leave it to the reader.

But if such knowledge is, I will not say too high for us, but clearly impossible, then 'objective rightness' *is* what we *think* objective, and we are left with 'subjective rightness.' And, in the teeth of his own doctrine, Mr. Sidgwick *himself accepts this conclusion.*

'Thus upon any theory of Ethics we require to distinguish *real* from *believed*, or as is now more commonly said "objective" from "subjective" rightness. Indeed this distinction sometimes involves us in a practical perplexity, not as regards our own conduct (for we obviously cannot distinguish what we believe to be right from what really is so) but in arguing with others.' (182.)

'For a Utilitarian must hold that it is always wrong and irrational for a man to do anything else than what he believes most conducive to Universal Happiness, and it is not possible for him to do more.' (456.)

The difference in the end is between what *we* think right and what others think it, and, on our author's view, what is that more than a 'subjective criterion?' 'But no subjective criterion of duty, however important it may be, can help us to construct a system of objective rules of conduct' (184).

This is what we wanted to show, that a one-sided view has proved fatal to itself, that the attempt to make right 'objective' in abstraction from the individual, has issued in the confession that right is 'subjective,' and individual judgment the practical criterion.

And now a word in conclusion. The reader may say, Then *is* not right merely subjective, and is not that contrary to the moral consciousness? I think it is contrary, but it is not my doctrine. For me, though right is subjective, it is none the less objective; but rather it is one just so far as it is the other. It is *both*, not in the sense that this or that man or set of men, as such, *make* it, nor in the sense that what *is* objectively right is simply taken up by the subjective side, and so *becomes* also (formally) subjective, but that right is a whole which is determined by both elements, and apart from either is not itself. I cannot further explain this here.

And again if I am asked, But does not the doctrine you hold admit of collisions of duties and exceptions to rules, and is not that Jesuitry? Would it not in fact be pernicious in practice?—my answer is very simple, that for me Ethics is not practical, but is a purely speculative science. I do not for one moment wish to blink the fact that in my opinion Ethics must teach that whereby the moral consciousness may be offended, and I have never attempted to blink it (see Eth. Stud. 143). *But* a practical collision between Ethics and morality is for me a sheer impossibility, because the former has nothing whatever to do with practice. The question for me is solely, ' Is moral science *true?* Has it or has it not succeeded in understanding the *facts* of morality?'

The truth or falsehood of this science are not to be decided by a direct appeal to the moral consciousness. This is supreme in its own sphere, as the experience which gives facts, but it cannot leave that sphere without altering its nature and losing its authority. Theory stands and falls by the theoretical test alone, i. e. its agreement with the facts and with itself. It is to start from and be verified in experience, but it is *not* mere experience. It is reflection and interpretation; and when mere experience pronounces on the abstract conclusions of science, then it ceases to be experience and, becoming theory, must itself stand and fall by the theoretical test.

But when science ceases to understand, and proposes to alter the facts, then common experience has a right to be heard, and the more loudly it speaks the better for all parties. For Mr. Sidgwick moral science is practical Casuistry which, if it does *not* alter the facts of life, has no title to existence. And here in my opinion the province of non-theoretical morality is invaded, and it has a right to speak. Science (to repeat it) is absolutely free while it is theory, while it keeps to the ὄν, and what is called 'common sense' is simply out of court. But when it becomes art, and applies itself to γενέσιν, then it must answer for itself and not fall back on the privileges of theory. Thus in morals against a theoretical dissection or construction of morality, however abhorrent to our feelings, we can properly claim no right but that of scientific discussion; but against any practical proposal we have a right to speak as practical moral agents.

I hope the reader will not go away with the idea that I wish to represent our author as a revolutionary character, or his book as 'dangerous for young persons.' I do not suppose there is any serious or, I might say, any difference of opinion between us as to what in particular is right and wrong, for we both substantially accept the doctrines of ordinary morality. The difference is one of principle, not detail. I object not to the things he teaches us to do, but to the spirit and the way in which he teaches us to do them. It is not the particular conclusions of his Casuistry, but the whole principle of it, that seems to me both false in theory and corrupt in practice.

And if we consider not our author himself but his main doctrine, we must say more. Deduced by a man of practical good sense, the conclusions of the hedonistic Art of Life would never seriously conflict with common morality. There are good psychological reasons for that. But once admit the principle, and what is to happen if men with no sense nor hold on real life, but gifted with a logical faculty, begin systematically to deduce from this slippery principle? Is this not a danger, and is it a wholly imaginary danger?

§ 9.—*The Final Difficulty.*

'And yet we cannot but admit ... that it is ultimately reasonable to seek one's own happiness' (473). I confess that, prepared as I was by a passage on p. 374, and though I saw that our author was but half-hearted in his attitude towards Egoism, I did not expect this. Here it is, however, and there can be no doubt about it. But 'whatever I judge to be Good, I cannot reasonably think that it is abstractly and primarily right that I should have it more than another' (366). 'In fact I have defined "reason" so that "reasonable" conduct must mean "right" or what "ought to be done"' (29), and right is 'the same for all minds or subjects' (182). This again has been the constant theme, and the nerve of the main argument. How did we suppress the egoist but by this? And now why did we knock down the egoist at all if we meant to set him up again? I must suppose that Mr. Sidgwick holds that 'reason' gives us two contradictory reports; and having used one throughout his book[1] he now brings forward the other. The previous argument then rests on a thesis the contradictory of which is no less true. If that is so, it may perhaps not be presumptuous to suggest that we might have been clearly informed of it before. It looks very much as if our author, after all his efforts, finds the egoistic position too strong for him, and is willing, if only it can be accomplished, to avoid the 'conflict between the two kinds of reasonableness' (374) by subordinating everything to the selfish end. The reader must judge whether, if this is so, a large and important part of the work must not be seriously modified, and whether at last 'practical reason' means anything at all.

Well, so much seems pretty clear, that it is reasonable to seek *both* one's own maximum pleasure *and* that of the creation; and the problem is to satisfy both desires at once. The question seems not so much about what ought to be as about the consistency of the Practical Reason (470-1). If the Good (sc. pleasure) of the individual is not ultimately identified with Universal Good (sc. pleasure), then the universe (471) is fundamentally irrational and morally chaotic.

In other words, it is 'a matter of life and death to the Practical Reason' (371) to show that the only true selfishness is morality, and morality the one best selfish policy.

The solution of the contradiction, which brings order out

---

[1] There is an exception on p. 473. Cf. supra, p. 7, note, and p. 36, note.

of chaos, is that certain quantities of pleasure and pain should be attached to individuals, that they should be adequately rewarded for obeying the rule of duty and punished for violating it (470).

The difficulty is as to how this attachment of pleasure and pain is to be effected. Humanity, we find, cannot wholly carry out the task, and hence something external to humanity is required. What remains then? Surely, surely it is our old friend the *Deus ex machina*[1], and anxiously we sit awaiting him: the crisis is at hand, the actors at a dead lock and we on the stretch. Vain expectation, for the days of Paley are gone by. The machine is grown old, and the God will not come to the front, and the stage is in confusion, and the curtain falls hurriedly in the middle of the fifth act.

As to the moral and religious character of Mr. Sidgwick's doctrine I have said what I thought necessary elsewhere. What I think he should make plainer is whether he thinks the above hypothesis removes evil from the universe; how this is possible while human beings remain on the one hand so stupid, and on the other hand so impulsive; and, supposing moral evil is not removed, whether 'Practical Reason' is satisfied with that. Next, what does he mean by *adequate* reward and what does he mean by punishment? Is the pain merely to be threatened? Will that serve? Surely we are much too stupid. Is it to be inflicted? Why? What good does that do? Is not that *immoral*? And what reward is adequate? We know what coin the 'Wages of Virtue' are to be paid in, but the amount surely matters, and the rules of payment for work; for may we not after all be dealt with unfairly? I do not know what our author's answer to these questions is, or whether he thinks they need an answer. I am of opinion that if hedonistic Moral Theology is to stand, they must be answered, and also that they cannot be answered.

[1] Mr. Sidgwick wishes to justify both selfishness and morality. The way to do it is to show that they are one thing from different points of view. He fails to effect any union from the internal nature of each, and so requires them to be brought together from the outside. That is a purely mechanical expedient.

And yet we cannot in fairness leave the matter here. We should wrong our author if we took him at his word, and judged him to mean no more than he says. His difficulty, we must believe, is other than he thinks it, and it is the old puzzle, How can morality be reconciled to the world?

The hardest form of the question, the problem of evil and the moral ought, is, I think, not what Mr. Sidgwick contemplates, nor again that of the general coincidence of happiness and virtue. What he has in his mind we take to be the familiar stumbling-block that in the world we know each man *is* not happy according as he is virtuous, and that he *ought* to be so because he deserves to be so. This is a knot which more than one philosopher has called on God and immortality to loose or to sever, and we think this was the real *dignus vindice nodus* with Mr. Sidgwick. It is indeed no matter to treat lightly, but a serious and difficult problem. I do not pretend to give a satisfactory solution, but, even though I overstep the limits of my undertaking, I will offer some remarks.

First of all, it is necessary to remember that in healing an evil there is a risk of 'healing it by another,' and that this is specially the case in a doctrine of rewards and punishments. Seeking to satisfy morality we may postulate that which itself is morally offensive, and I think this has certainly been done in some forms of the doctrine of rewards and punishments[1], though I am far from suggesting that it is so with all. But I am not going to enter on this point.

I think the simplest plan is to go to the moral consciousness and ask the question, Do I deserve a reward for doing my duty? Do I deserve punishment for moral offences? If punishment and reward are taken to consist in mere pain or pleasure attached to me from without, I cannot find that morality tells me I deserve *either*. But if they are taken to mean the lowering or heightening of my private life, then

---

[1] Here is a specimen. 'I shall therefore dismiss my reader with this maxim, viz., Our Happiness in this World proceeds from the Suppression of our Desires, but in the next World from the Gratification of them.' Spectator, No. 634.

I understand it to say that I do deserve punishment, but not that I deserve reward.

My bad will is what ought not to be, and the negation of that will is demanded, though mere feeling of pain is not. But the assertion of the good in me to the suppression of the bad entails lowering of my private existence, contradiction and pain. It may entail, *supposing* that to be the only way to assert the good, even my extinction, and so this may be demanded.

The heightening of my existence as *mine* I cannot see that morality does demand necessarily. Calling for the assertion of good in me it does call for the assertion of my existence. But I cannot find that it says to me, Your existence *ought* to be increased with increase of the good. On the other hand it does say, You must assert the good to the extinction of your existence, *if* that is the way to assert the good.

So much seems fairly clear: but then the real question is, I think, not, Does morality say this? but Does it not *also* say something more, and something perhaps not agreeing with this? Do we not feel when we see wickedness flourish and virtue in rags, This is not right, or good, or just? No doubt we do. And then must we not say that it is just or good or right that advantage should go with virtue, and disadvantage with vice, not merely on the whole but in each individual agent, and that a world, where it is not so, is not governed morally?

It would no doubt be possible, taking a position of extreme rigour, to call in the name of morality for the suppression of these sentiments: but that we feel would be a one-sided and unsatisfactory view of the case.

There can be no doubt that the demand for rewards as well as punishments rests on a true moral judgment ('instinct' or 'intuition' if you will). But I think it is a mistake to suppose that this demand is absolute. The error of the moral or theological doctrine we are discussing is, I think, first that it maintains in an unqualified manner that which is nowhere true apart from a higher truth, and secondly, that, by a false or uncertain analogy, it asserts the conditions of life as we know them in human society to be valid beyond that society. But this is to anticipate the conclusion.

Let us ask then, Is it just that unequal happiness should go with equal virtue? The preliminary answer to that is, *If* there is a law which assigns advantage and disadvantage in proportion to virtue and vice, then you deserve both, and it is unjust if you do not have them [1].

This is not much more than a verbal answer, and I give it to call attention to the meaning of justice. The real question is not, Is it *just* that there should be a moral law for assigning advantage and disadvantage? for that, I think, has no meaning at all. It is, *Ought* advantage and disadvantage to be assigned? *Is* there an absolute moral law to that effect? And if so, does it not remain unexecuted? If you or I were the ruler of the universe, should we not think it *immoral* to govern it as it is governed? That is the real question. Should we not have a law to reward virtue and vice, and should we not act on it?

I think we make a mistake if we affirm this, and the mistake, as we said, consists partly in an unfounded analogy, and partly in an incomplete analogy. We take the analogy of human society, and then we emphasise one moral law which holds there, forgetting wholly the highest law. I will take the latter point first.

(1) If you or I were the ruler of a finite human community, should we feel morally bound always to assign disadvantage and advantage in proportion to moral evil and good? Should we feel bound always to reward virtue? I do not think so, but for the present let us say, Yes, we will

---

[1] I must ask leave here to correct a mistake I have made elsewhere (Eth. Stud. 191, note). I denied that getting one's deserts and getting justice were the same thing. Of course in real justice they are not the same, but then in ideal justice they are, and I cannot now understand how I failed to see this. In fact, one's desert is what is due to one by law : it is advantage or disadvantage necessarily connected with our acts by virtue of a law. The execution of such a law is justice, and hence 'what is just' and 'what I deserve' are two names of one thing. It follows that there is no desert where there is no law; and it follows again that *if* the highest moral law is *not* a law providing for the distribution of advantage and disadvantage, then the conceptions of justice and desert are inapplicable there and must be overruled.

reward virtue and punish vice proportionably by an absolute law. Now I ask, *Why* should we do this? And for myself I answer, We do this because by doing this we realize the greatest amount of good (not pleasure)[1]. But having said this, I begin to perceive that this law cannot be absolute. We are the servants of the law in one way; in another way, by identifying ourselves with the highest law, Do the most good, we override all lower laws and become their masters. Human life being as it is, we do most good by having rewards and punishments generally; and again, for the sake of the good, we are obliged (for obvious reasons) to go by a law. But then, all that being admitted, it does not follow that we may never go by another law which overrules the former.

And now I put it to you, if you were ruler, whether you would have an absolute law to reward virtue proportionably, or whether you would do it without a law. If the latter, how do you justify it? If the former, then are you not speaking of what *might* be best if the world were not the world it is, but rather what you wish it to be? Does not experience show that such a law would not be moral as things are, because it would do more harm than good?

I think we can easily see that we might have a state of society in which, if the ruler tried to distribute advantage and disadvantage by merit, he would produce on the whole less virtue and more vice. If so, what is it moral to do? Surely to go on the absolute law to do good, and to override all relative laws. Surely the law of retribution is one of these relative laws.

Morality, it seems to me, not only can but does approve of such a proceeding. No rational community tries to go by an absolute law of rewards and punishments. They all exercise for instance the right of pardon, because they do not believe that justice is the highest moral law. And morality sanctions what they do.

---

[1] Mr. Sidgwick does not yet (Mind, V. 32) seem to be aware that a man may be 'prepared to accept 'Common Good' as the ultimate end for which moral rules exist,' and yet reject Hedonism.

It is the old matter of collision of duties. For morality I am sure no law is absolutely imperative except the law, Realize the good; and *all* other laws must in theory be subordinate to this. In practice I do not say *all* are, because a collision may never be able to take place, but in practice again I am sure that this law of rewards and punishments is subordinated. In fact the highest moral law, before which all others must bow, is not justice; it does not directly distribute advantage and disadvantage to the individual, and stands above such a consideration.

Of course it must be understood that I am speaking of the world and morality as we know them. I recognize no other criterion. The world of our fancies and wishes, the home of absolute categorical imperatives, has no place in legitimate speculation.

What it comes to then, so far, is this. In human communities it is unjust not to reward and punish where there is a law to do so. It is right to have such a law where by doing so you realize most good. Otherwise it would not be right to have such a law. And where you have such a law it may be right to override it. Yes, I will say it, there *is* a duty to be unjust.

(2) If this is true, then the analogy as we had it was left incomplete. And moreover, in the second place, it is unfounded. I do not see how we have the means of judging from that which we do in human communities for the sake of the good, to that which is good and right to be done in the universe. We do not, and is it sceptical to add? we cannot fully know the conditions there. If any one wishes to maintain that *because* advantage and disadvantage do not coincide with virtue and vice, *therefore* the government of the world is not moral, he must be prepared to show that, if he were in power, he could produce less evil and more good than there is, by going on a law of rewards and punishments. In other language, supposing that in all cases the self-realization of each man as such were proportionate to the identification of his will with the will of the whole—would the will of the whole system be more intensely realized in fuller individuals?

I do not see how any man is to say, Yes; and, if he will not do that, his objection must fall.

The mere moral consciousness cannot pronounce on such questions as these. It sees its good and goods, and it knows its duty. Give it an hypothesis, an 'if,' and with care you may extract something from it; but it is a delicate matter to do so, for, if you put your case in the least one-sidedly, you are sure to get a wrong answer. And to turn an 'if' into an 'it is' is wholly beyond it. Let me remark in conclusion, that the reader who wishes to fall back on Omnipotence will find a good answer in Mr. Sidgwick, p. 469.

But from this theological discussion we cannot shut out religion. And, when we get there, it does seem that the notion of claiming reward for our merits and standing on our rights with God is a pre-Christian point of view, I had almost said an anachronism. We all know that one of the leading doctrines of Christianity is that not one man has any desert before the law, or can be justified except on his abnegation of every sort of claim. No one can deny that this is an important phenomenon of the religious consciousness, and I think it is not harsh to say that a theological discussion which overlooks or refuses to consider this fact as a fact, is a strangely one-sided account of the subject.

It is natural at the end of our examination to ask ourselves what we think of the argument as a whole. It would be idle if I said anything else than that, as an argument to prove a thesis, I believe it has no value. I can find no unity of principle which holds its parts together. Rather I seem everywhere to have seen an attempt to unite irreconcileable points of view, which has failed because the criticism, which should first have loosened their opposition, has been wanting. Hedonism and Individualism on the one side, and abstract Rationalism on the other, have met but have not come together, and the result is a mere syncretism, a mechanical mixture of both.

I make no pretence to estimate the worth of the Methods of Ethics as a whole, but I may say thus much, that, as we have found an absence of criticism in its leading ideas, so it is far from being a complete collection of opinion on the subjects of which it treats. And this failure to take account of the views most opposed to traditional English doctrine has been at least one cause of the uncertain handling of leading conceptions, and the confusion in the result. On the other hand there is no doubt that the work is valuable; and it is obvious that there are two things in it which for some time will keep their place,—the examination of popular morality and the discussions on English thought. No book, it is safe to say, has been published for years which has done so much to stimulate ethical speculation amongst us, and in more senses than one to point to a reform in our moral philosophy.

APPENDIX.

Note A.

Whether the sum is to be realized as a summed series I do not know; but in Mind (V. 37) Mr. Sidgwick writes as if this might be his opinion. In this article he subjects to 'summary treatment' the objection against the sum of pleasures as stated by Mr. Green. I shall not presume to say anything on Mr. Green's behalf, who is far better able to defend himself than I him. But as Mr. Sidgwick has mentioned my name in the matter, I may point out that he has not made any attempt to meet the objections I raised in my book. He may please himself as to doing this, but he should not write as if he had done what he has not done. I asked, Is the sum finite or infinite? He has not answered. I asked, Is the end realized in life or after death? He has not answered. He is silent on the question of approximation as the end; and if he answers the question whether the sum is a series in time or coexistent, it is impossible to say what his answer is (*vide* Eth. Stud. 88–9, and note). If our author wishes the issue to be clear, he must first take the trouble to find out what he means by greatest sum of pleasures as the end, and not leave to a critic the task of conjecturing his views before he examines them.

So far as what Mr. Sidgwick has said bears on the general question I will endeavour to say what is required, though I can do little more than repeat the remarks in the text.

And first let me say that the question is whether we can *get* the Hedonistic end, *not* whether we can *aim* at it, and that it is time our author realized this distinction rather more clearly. Next, if Mr. Sidgwick means by 'greatest' an infinite sum, I refer him to my book (70, 89). If he means a limited sum, then what he has to say seems to come to this. 'A finite greatest possible series in time can be summed, and hence greatest sum of pleasures may be gained, because the pleasures are had, though not all at once. And, again, the sum is a whole with parts, and you can have the whole by and in the parts.' (These of course are not his words.)

Now the question here is *not*, Can any finite series in time be considered as a whole with parts? The question is, (i) What does greatest possible sum mean? And, (ii) If the end is the realization of a series, can the end be realized *before* the series is summed? And if it is realized not before, is it realized at all?

(i) Mr. Sidgwick says 'we can aim at living as long as possible, without any regard to the manner of our living; and if we turn out centenarians, we shall commonly be thought to have succeeded in our aim' (37). This shows that our author has not even seen the difficulty. The assertion that A has lived as long as possible means, I should have thought, that under all the conditions, his will being one, a certain finite length of life was possible, and that he has lived it. The amount in comparison with other men is surely irrelevant, unless what is meant is that he has lived as long as it is possible for any human being to live, i.e. that there is a fixed maximum (say 100 years) which he has reached. If Mr. Sidgwick means this latter, and will also fix a maximum of pleasures, then I am quite ready to discuss such a view. But at present he has left us in the dark.

(ii) Next, if we make an end of living as long as possible, or an end of realizing the greatest possible amount of pleasure, can we attain these ends? and if so, how?

The end of living as long as possible is surely not gained until we die. The summing of the series is our extinction; and in and by that alone can we gain our object. So with the sum of pleasures. It may be said of a man, He got the sum of pleasures; but it cannot be said till all his pleasures are over. If a man said, 'I want long life,' when he was old he would have got it. If he says, 'I want a great sum of pleasure in my life,' again a time may come when he can say, not 'I have it,' but 'I have had it.' But if he says 'longest' and 'greatest,' he is foredoomed to disappointment.

But the Good must surely be κτητὸν ἀνθρώπῳ. Surely it must be that which I can say I have now, not wait for until I am dead. Surely, again, to have had as much pleasure in life as possible is an object I never can say is mine. And is it not a mockery to tell us, You shall have the end of your being when you have ceased to be: the end is not to have but to have had; and when that comes you are gone?

Does it help us if we bring in the conception of whole and parts? Not in the least. It is the same thing over again. To say of a limited number of pleasures or days, This is part of the whole and so I realize the whole in this, is simply suicidal. For *any* number of moments or pleasures, no matter how small, are a 'part' of the sum; and the dilemma we are left with is as above. Either the end is realized in a part of the series, or it is realized only in the whole, which is not a whole till the series is summed. If the first is true then the end is *not* the sum; if the last is true *we* never get the end.

If this is not plain I am afraid I cannot make it plain. Let us say once more, The object of my life, my object in my life, is to live the greatest possible number of days. Do I, can I ever get for myself that object? Is it not to turn my life into the aim for a success which cannot come, to make life 'Death's fool,' a perpetual dying, where there is loss in every gain, and the end we live for, once gained, means in that moment the loss of all?

It is so with the pursuit of pleasure. If you will not put a limit to that which you want you never will get it. You never will be able to say, I have it. You never will be able even to say, I have had it. If this is not to aim at the unattainable, what is? And if my good is unattainable by me, is it good at all?

And now when we leave the individual, as we must if we are to follow Mr. Sidgwick, does not every difficulty become still more difficult? The series of the pleasures of the sentient world is to be a whole with parts. If the end is to get a part, then *any* part is the end. If the end is to get the whole series, the series of the pleasures of the sentient world must be summed. Then I grant you the end has been, in one sense, attained; but I should like to ask, When does the time come? and who is it that gets, or has got the end?

The end as a coexisting aggregate has been considered in the text; and in ending this note I will ask the reader to believe that it is not for my own pleasure that I have wearied both him and myself with the subject.

Note B.

What does *objective* mean for Mr. Sidgwick?

(i) It is opposed to 'the sensations of the sentient being which may vary from A to B without either being in error' (23, cf. 24). A judgment is not objective when you cannot raise the question of error (183; I abstain from criticism). But this so far tells us only what the objective is *not*.

(ii) There is a comparatively rare use by which it = that which I perceive as *not* my feeling self. 'Attitude of our minds' may be 'objective, extra-regarding rather than introspective,' i. e. directed not on pleasures but 'external objects and particular activities' (133). It is opposed to 'the emotion that accompanies his cognition of this relation,' i. e. to some law or ideal represented as objective (371, cf. 24). In this sense however the objective seems indifferent to truth or error.

(iii) The next sense is, What is valid for all subjects? and at first it seems as if we might say, What I judge to be so valid (366). 'The objective judgment "that an end is good."' But here if I am wrong my judgment would be subjective merely, and we see that the true objective = what *is* valid for all subjects, and in this sense it seems = the subjectively necessary or normal. This perhaps is Mr. Sidgwick's most common usage.

Ought is objective; and 'this notion of "ought" . . . we may perhaps say, is a necessary form of our moral apprehension' (93). So beauty and 'the so-called secondary qualities of matter' are objective (24) because error is possible. In this sense the objective is opposed to what *we* like. It is 'an object of knowledge and as such the same for all minds,' and so has 'objective existence' (5). It is a 'standard' (96, cf. 187).

And in this signification of necessary or normal we could 'distinguish *real* from *believed*, or, as is now commonly said, "objective" from "subjective" rightness' (182, cf. 190, note); and understand 'that Right and Wrong are really objective: that is, the same, whether recognised or not, for all Minds or Subjects' (182). But Mr. Sidgwick means more than this by the term.

(iv). It = what is real apart from consciousness. It is the 'external aspect and relations' of an act (182): 'objective relations of the conscious subject, when distinguished in reflective analysis from the consciousness accompanying and resulting from them' (371): 'the relation between the mind and something else, which is whatever it is independently of our cognition of it' (370): 'objective constitution of the relations of conscious beings' (375). And so we have 'Objective Good,' *v.* 'Subjective Good or Happiness' (377).

We see, from p. 381, that this is the meaning of 'externally or objectively right' conduct: and must so interpret the opposition (182) of 'real' and 'believed,' and the objective character of Right and Wrong. This again seems meant when it is said (184) that 'no subjective criterion of duty, however important it may be, can help us to construct a system of objective rules of conduct.' And the 'objective rule or imperative' (62) may be something which is, whatever it is, out of relation to the mind.

I think it would have made things clearer if Mr. Sidgwick had been more explicit as to the meaning of this term. May I venture to refer him to Mr. Wallace's Logic of Hegel, p. 73?